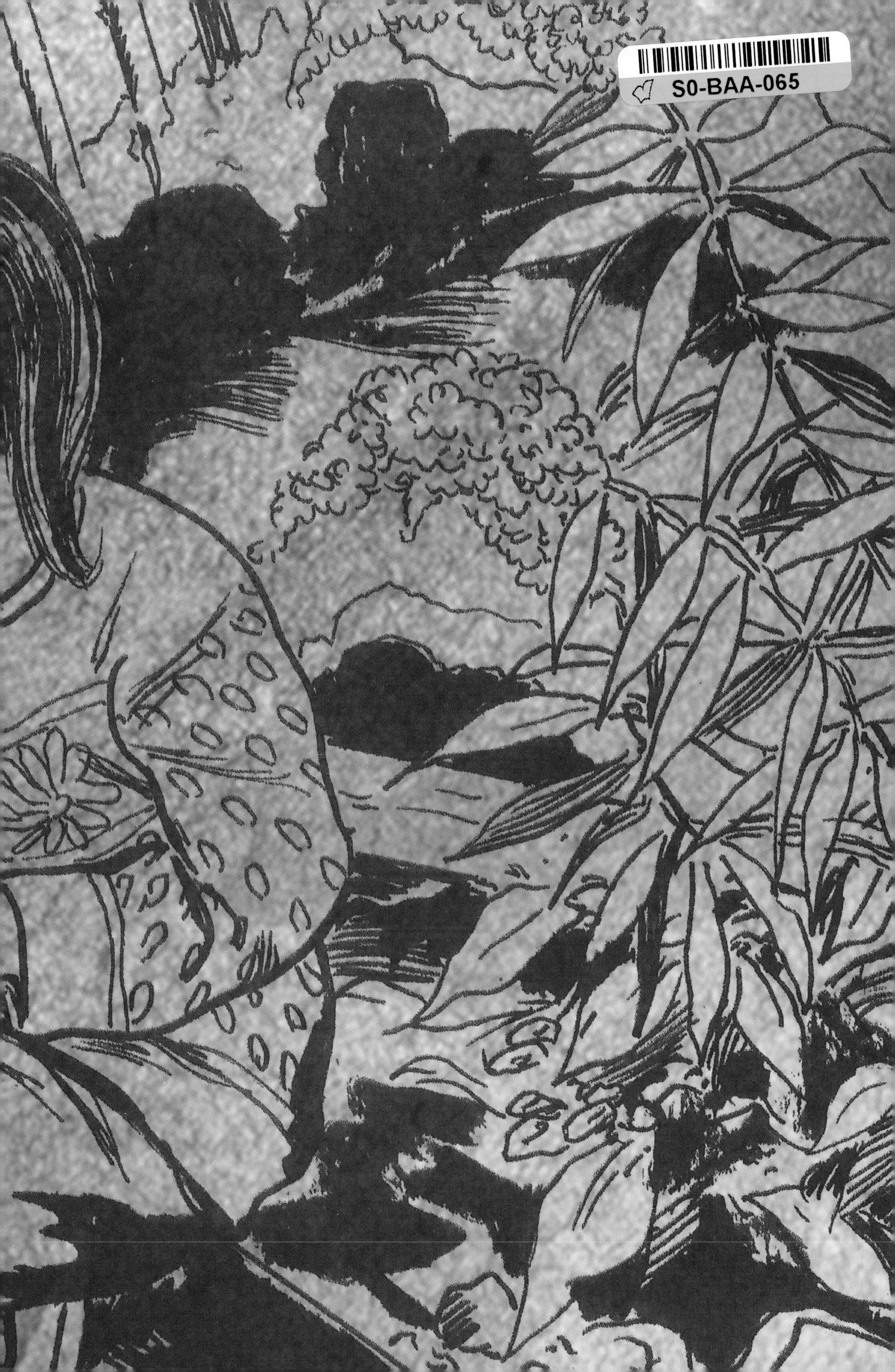

*For my son Crosby, my sister June and my dear friends
Laura McCarthy and Catherine Dauxerre.*

**Written and colored by Marguerite Van Cook
Adapted and drawn by James Romberger**

**Editor and Associate Publisher: Eric Reynolds
Book Design: Tony Ong
Production: Paul Baresh
Publisher: Gary Groth**

FANTAGRAPHICS BOOKS, INC.
Seattle, Washington, USA

ISBN 978-1-60699-789-5

First printing: November, 2014
Printed in Malaysia

THE

LATE CHILD

AND OTHER ANIMALS

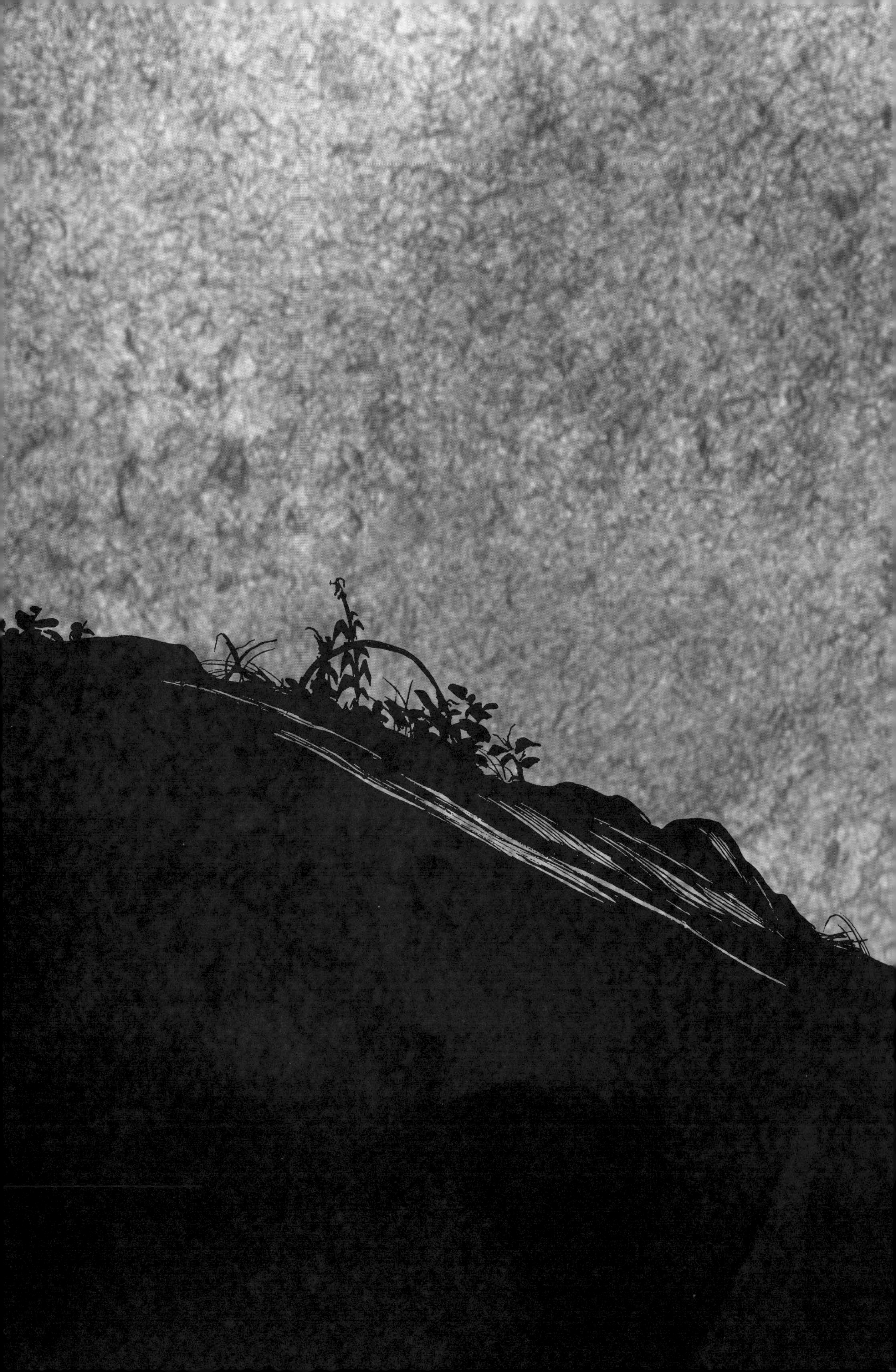

MARGUERITE VAN COOK
JAMES ROMBERGER

THE

LATE CHILD

AND OTHER ANIMALS

FANTAGRAPHICS BOOKS, INC.
SEATTLE, WA

HETTY'S WAR

THE SISTERS WATCHED PORTSMOUTH BURN.

LOOK, HETTY. THEY'VE GOT ALL THROUGH QUEEN STREET.

CAN YOU SEE IF MUM AND DAD HAVE BEEN HIT?

NO, DAISY.

5

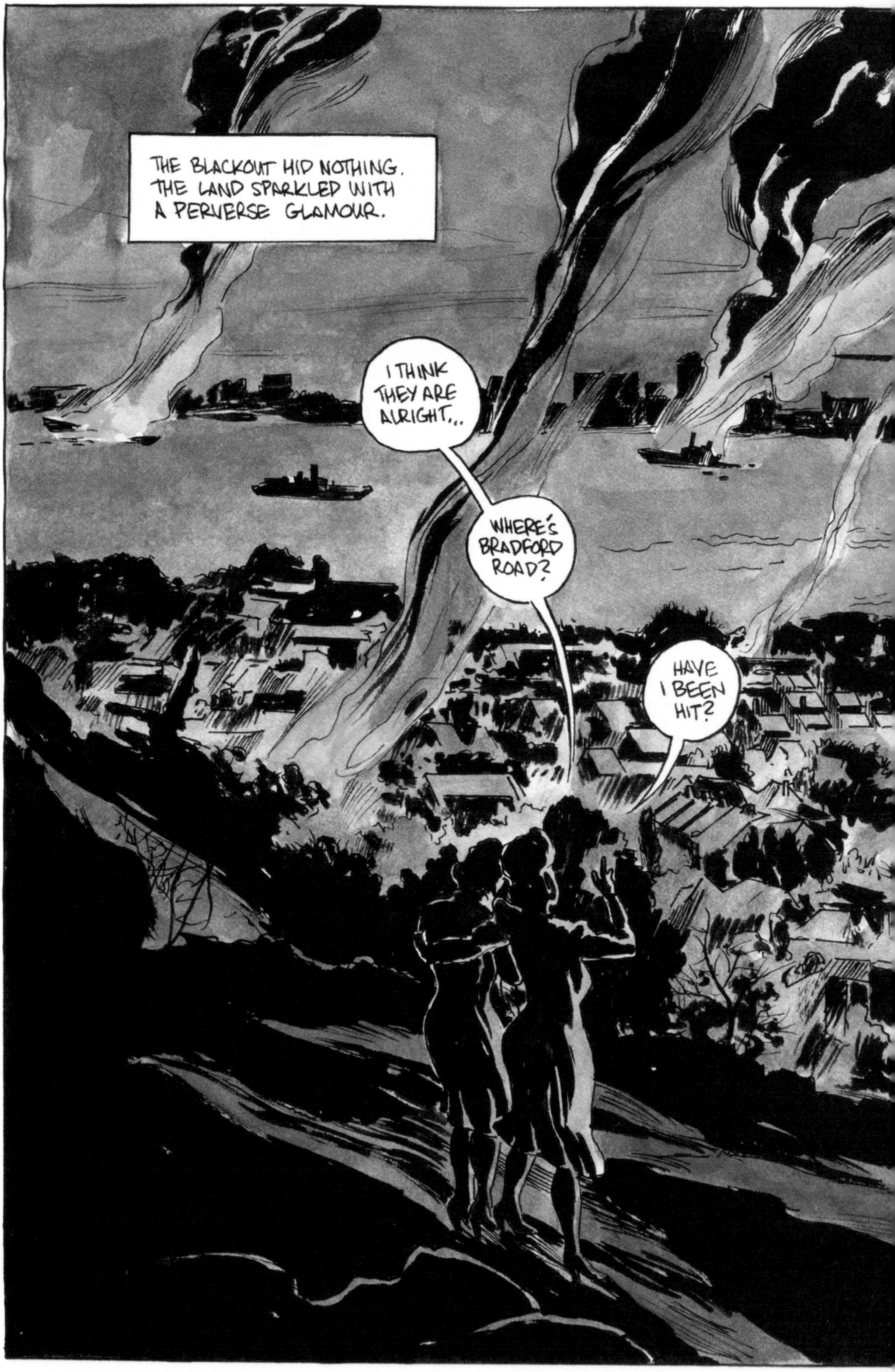
THE BLACKOUT HID NOTHING. THE LAND SPARKLED WITH A PERVERSE GLAMOUR.
I THINK THEY ARE ALRIGHT...
WHERE'S BRADFORD ROAD?
HAVE I BEEN HIT?

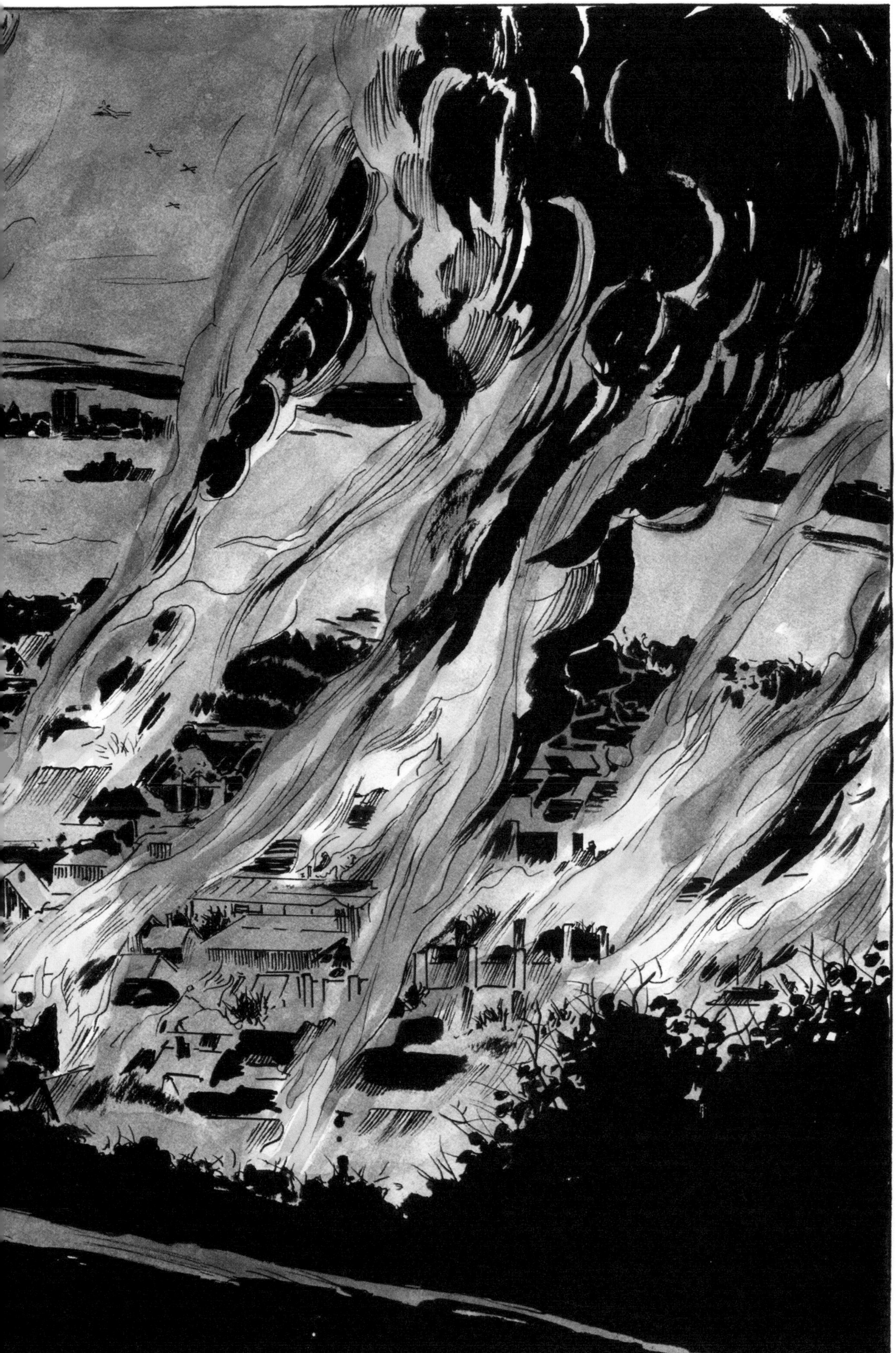

THE SIRENS SOUNDED THE ALL CLEAR.

AS DAWN BEGAN TO BREAK, THE FLAMES WERE DIMMED BY THE BRUISED COMPLEXION OF THE SKY.

WELL, THIS WON'T DO.

I'D BETTER GET HOME AND SEE WHAT IS GOING ON.

I MUST SEE HOW NELLIE, MUM, AND DAD ARE...

IF ANYTHING HAS HAPPENED TO THEM.

NELLIE WAS THE THIRD AND YOUNGEST SISTER.

ANYWAY, FREDDIE MUST BE SO FRIGHTENED!

"RED SKY AT NIGHT, SHEPHERD'S DELIGHT, RED SKY IN THE MORNING, SHEPHERD'S WARNING."

IT WOULD CERTAINLY RAIN TODAY, AND THEN THE PEOPLE WHO HAD BEEN HIT WOULD HAVE AN EVEN WORSE TIME.

OH, HET. DO YOU THINK YOU'LL BE ABLE TO GET ALL THE WAY TO MUM'S?

FREDDIE WAS THEIR ELDER BROTHER.

A CHILDHOOD FEVER HAD LEFT HIM SIMPLE.

THE TWO LEGGY GIRLS HALF RAN AS THE STEEP INCLINE FORCED THEM TO PICK UP SPEED.

THEY WOULD TRY TO SALVAGE THIS AND THAT, ASSESS THE DAMAGE, CRY, COMMISERATE, AND PUT UP A GOOD FRONT, ALL AT THE SAME TIME.

DAISY TURNED OFF AT THE BAKER'S TO TRY TO CATCH THE EARLY BREAD.

SOMETIMES, THEY POOLED THEIR RESOURCES TO GET A WHOLE LOAF.

THEY SAID A WEIGHTED GOODBYE.

NONE OF THEIR SIBLING DIFFERENCES MEANT ANYTHING NOW.

DAISY LIKED HER CREATURE COMFORTS, BUT NEITHER GIRL THOUGHT FOR A SECOND THAT SHE SHOULD HAVE PREFERENTIAL TREATMENT OVER ANYONE ELSE.

IN PLACES, WHOLE STREETS WERE GONE.

IN OTHERS, BLOWN-AWAY WALLS LEFT THE INTERIOR WALLS EXPOSED, LIKE GIANT DOLLHOUSES.

ALL OF THE INTIMACIES OF DAILY LIFE WERE LEFT HANGING IN TIME.

HETTY NEVER CUT ACROSS THE NON-OPEN BOMBSITES. IT WAS ALL TOO EASY TO TRIGGER A BOMB THAT HADN'T DETONATED.

SOME OF THIS HAD HAPPENED WEEKS BEFORE, NIGHTS BEFORE...

EVERY NIGHT, THERE WAS SOME NEWLY DONE-FOR HOUSE.

THE END OF A DREAM FOR SOMEONE.

THEY COULD STICK THIS OUT, THOUGH. HITLER? TO HELL WITH HIM. THE BUDDLEIA BUSHES STILL MANAGED TO SCRAMBLE THROUGH THE RUBBLE.

THEY SPLAYED ACROSS THE BRICKS IN TOTAL DEFIANCE.

JUST BECAUSE EVERYTHING WAS A MESS, THERE WAS NO REASON SHE SHOULD LOOK A FRIGHT.

I HAVEN'T GOT IT ANY WORSE THAN ANYONE ELSE.

AND I'M BETTER OFF THAN MOST.

AT NORTH END...

DID LANDPORT GET HIT BAD?

NO, DUCKS. THEY'RE ALRIGHT ALL ALONG THEYER.

BUT VEY 'AD A TERRIBLE TOYME DOWEN AWOUND VICTOWIA PAWRK.

IF ANYTHING HAD HAPPENED TO HER MUM, OR NELLIE, OR FRED...

SHE DECIDED TO SKIP HER OWN HOUSE AND GO STRAIGHT TO HER FATHER'S.

AND NOW IT BEGAN TO RAIN. THERE WAS NO END TO IT.

13

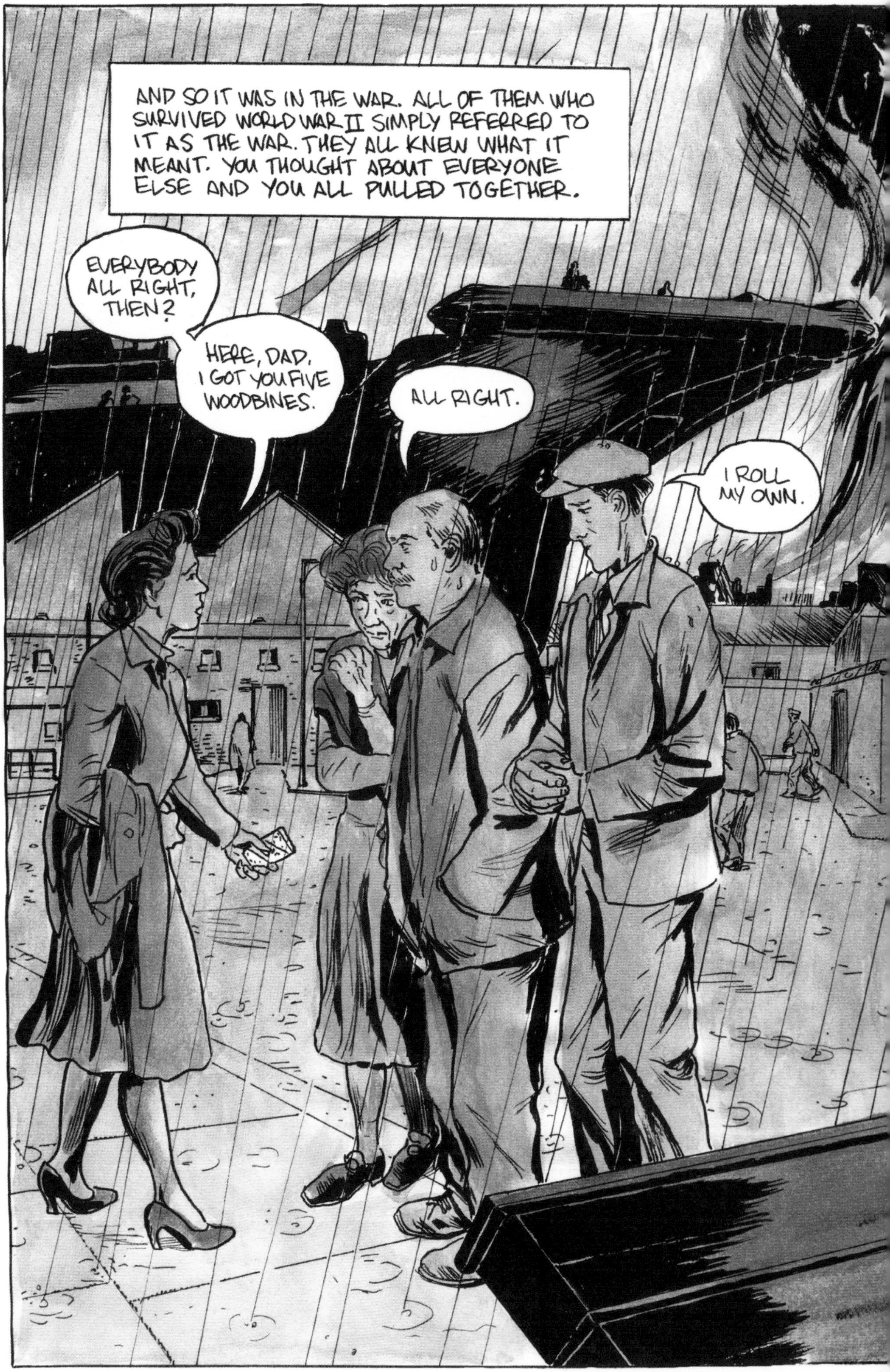
AND SO IT WAS IN THE WAR. ALL OF THEM WHO SURVIVED WORLD WAR II SIMPLY REFERRED TO IT AS THE WAR. THEY ALL KNEW WHAT IT MEANT. YOU THOUGHT ABOUT EVERYONE ELSE AND YOU ALL PULLED TOGETHER.
EVERYBODY ALL RIGHT, THEN?
HERE, DAD, I GOT YOU FIVE WOODBINES.
ALL RIGHT.
I ROLL MY OWN.

IN SOME WAYS,
THOSE TIMES HAD
BEEN VERY SPECIAL.

HETTY'S FRED HAD SIGNED UP WITHOUT A THOUGHT.

SHE KEPT HIS LITTLE WATERCOLOR FOLDED UP JUST AS IT HAD COME IN THE LETTER.

HE TOO WAS CALLED FRED, LIKE HER DAD AND HER BROTHER. FUNNY, REALLY.

HE DID A REALLY LOVELY JOB OF CAPTURING ALL OF THE FLOWERS.

ALONG THE BACK WALL WERE THE HOLLYHOCKS, HUGGING THE TRELLIS WHERE THEY HAD THE MOST SUN.

ABOVE THEM, CLUMPS OF HONEYSUCKLE HAD MASSED BUSILY. THEN, GERANIUMS AND GLADIOLI.

AND IN FRONT OF THEM, BRIGHT SWEET-SMELLING WALLFLOWERS FOUGHT FOR SPACE WITH THE SWEET WILLIAMS.

THEY WEREN'T THE MOST BEAUTIFUL TO LOOK AT, BUT OH, THEY HAD SMELLED SO LOVELY.

THAT WAS BEFORE SHE HAD LOST HER SENSE OF SMELL. SOMETHING PSYCHOSOMATIC, THEY HAD SAID, BUT SHE COULD STILL REMEMBER THE GORGEOUS SCENTS.

IN FRONT OF THEM, ANTIRRHINUMS GREW PLAYFULLY; BUNNY RABBITS, THEY CALLED THEM.

EACH LITTLE FLOWER COULD BE MADE TO SNAP OPEN. SOME PEOPLE CALLED THEM SNAPDRAGONS, BUT THAT SEEMED TOO HARSH FOR THE WEE VELVETY HEADS.

UP TOWARDS THE END WAS A CHAMOMILE BED WITH ITS TINY DAISIES. THEY REMINDED HER OF HER MUM AND HER SISTER, BOTH MARGUERITES, ALTHOUGH THEY CALLED HER SISTER BY THE DIMINUTIVE DAISY.

FRED HAD PLANTED THE BRIGHT BLUE LOBELIA THAT EDGED THE PATH HIMSELF. AND THERE IT WAS, CAPTURED FOREVER IN THE BRUSH STROKES ON THE PAGE.

IT WAS AS IF HE'D REMEMBERED EVERY PETAL; THEY WERE EACH SO CAREFULLY PUT DOWN.

THE MARKS STILL LOOKED WET.

YOU COULD SEE HIS HAND.

AND THEY HAD BEEN SO HAPPY, SHE AND FRED.

THEY HAD DECIDED TO ADOPT A BABY.

HE WAS IN NORTH AFRICA WHEN HE HAD PAINTED THE PICTURE.

SHE KNEW THAT NOW, FAR AWAY FROM THE RAINY DAY THAT MADE THEIR GARDEN GO GREEN, HE WAS IN THE NASTY DRY DESERT DRIVING A LORRY.

IT WAS A MIRACLE THAT HE HAD BEEN ABLE TO MAKE THIS JEWEL-LIKE PAINTING.

AND THEN THE MIRACLE WAS ALL THE GREATER THAT IT HAD COME ALL THE WAY TO HER.

THE CENSORS BLOCKED OUT SO MUCH OF THEIR LETTERS THAT IN THE END THE DRAWINGS WERE BETTER.

IT HELPED KEEP THEIR CHINS UP.

HE PROBABLY DIDN'T WANT TO WORRY HER OR GET TOO EMOTIONAL, EITHER.

BUT HE ALWAYS MADE SURE TO WRITE HOW MUCH HE LOVED HER.

To Hetty,
the only girl
in the world,
I love you,
Fred

HE HAD BEEN VERY FUNNY TOO.

BUT SUCH A GOOD ARTIST.

ALWAYS SEEING THE LIGHT SIDE.

SHE WAS TOO TIRED TO GO TO THE BOMB SHELTER WHEN THE SIRENS WENT.

SHE STAYED IN BED.

A BOMB FELL THROUGH THE ROOF ONTO THE FLOOR NEXT TO HER.

NO TIME TO THINK, SHE JUST SCOOPED IT UP

AND THREW IT OUT THE WINDOW

THE BOMB WENT OFF IN THE YARD AND BLASTED THE GLASS INWARDS.

SHE SHELTERED BEHIND THE FOOTBOARD.

IT WAS A BRIGHT SUNNY MORNING WHEN THEY BEGAN TO TAKE ACCOUNT OF EVERYTHING.

HER LITTLE DOG BRANDY HAD BEEN IN HIS KENNEL IN THE BACKYARD.

HE HAD BEEN BLOWN HIGH IN THE AIR AND KILLED BY THE BLAST. POOR LITTLE THING. SHE WAS SO FOND OF IT.

THE GARDEN HAD GONE ALONG WITH THE DOG.

ALL DOWN THE STREET, PEOPLE HAD TAKEN VERY BAD HITS.

HETTY, HAVE YOU SEEN MY TALL BOY?

YOU KNOW THAT LOVELY CHEST I BOUGHT FROM HANDLEY'S. I GOT THE DRAWERS, BUT THE REST IS GONE.

THINGS WERE OFTEN DISPLACED AFTER A BOMBING, SOMETIMES TO SAVE THEM FROM BURNING.

I'LL ASK MRS. PARR.

HER OTHER NEIGHBOR WAS CLEANING UP HER GARDEN OF DEBRIS.

MRS. PARR!

MRS. HASTY HAS ALL THE DRAWERS, BUT SHE HAS LOST HER TALL BOY.

HAVE YOU SEEN IT?

MRS. PARR WAS A STRONG WOMAN WITH GOOD LUNGS.

THE WHOLE STREET FELL OUT.

MRS. PARR WAS A FRIEND.

BUT THOSE TIMES WERE WHEN THEY NEEDED TO LAUGH.

HETTY WENT TO THE CHILDREN'S WARD TO PICK A CHILD.

SHE AND FRED WANTED A LITTLE GIRL.

THERE WERE SO MANY CHILDREN THAT NEEDED HOMES, BUT THEY THOUGHT IT WOULD BE LOVELY TO HAVE A LITTLE GIRL AND DRESS HER UP AND IT WOULD BE A WONDERFUL WAY TO SHARE THEIR HAPPINESS. THE WHOLE IDEA OF PICKING A CHILD STRUCK HER AS AWFUL, BUT THE CASE WORKER SAID THERE WAS NO OTHER WAY TO GET THE BEST MATCH.

SO, THERE IT WAS.

ON THE WARD, THE NURSE WARNED HER ABOUT ONE BABY.

THAT ONE'S NOT PERFECT. SHE'S GOT A CYST ON HER NAVEL.

HETTY KNEW INSTANTLY THAT THAT BABY MUST GO HOME WITH HER. IT MADE HER ANGRY TO THINK ABOUT IT.

JUNE WAS A LOVELY LITTLE GIRL.

MY GOODNESS, IT MADE HER CROSS TO THINK ABOUT IT!

FUNNY THEY HAD MADE IT THROUGH THE WAR UNTIL IT WAS OVER, AND THAT WAS WHEN THE WORST HAPPENED.

JUNE'S SECOND BIRTHDAY HAD COME AND GONE, AND THE WAR HAD COME TO A CLOSE. THE LADS WERE COMING HOME.

THAT MORNING THE CONCLUDING ADOPTION PAPERS FOR FILING CAME IN THE POST. FOR THE PAST COUPLE OF YEARS THERE WERE VISITS FROM SOCIAL WORKERS AND ALL SORTS OF RED TAPE, BUT NOW THEY WERE READY TO FINALIZE THE ADOPTION.

SHE HAD LOVED THE LITTLE GIRL FROM THE FIRST MOMENT THAT SHE SAW HER.

AFTER TWO YEARS, THE SUN SHONE WHEN SHE OPENED HER PRETTY BLUE EYES, AND SHE COULDN'T WAIT FOR FRED TO COME HOME AND THEIR LIVES TO TRULY BEGIN TOGETHER.

HETTY WAS THRILLED.

SHE WAS ABOUT TO LEAVE TO FINISH THE FILING.

JUNE'S BEAUTIFUL HAIR HUNG DOWN IN BRAIDS, LIKE STRINGS OF PEARLS, SHINY AND ORDERED.

THE PRECIOUS CHILD'S SMALL TEETH WERE WHITE AND STRONG AND SHE HAD THE MOST ADORABLE SMILE.

MWAH!

AS SHE OPENED THE DOOR

THE WORLD FELL APART

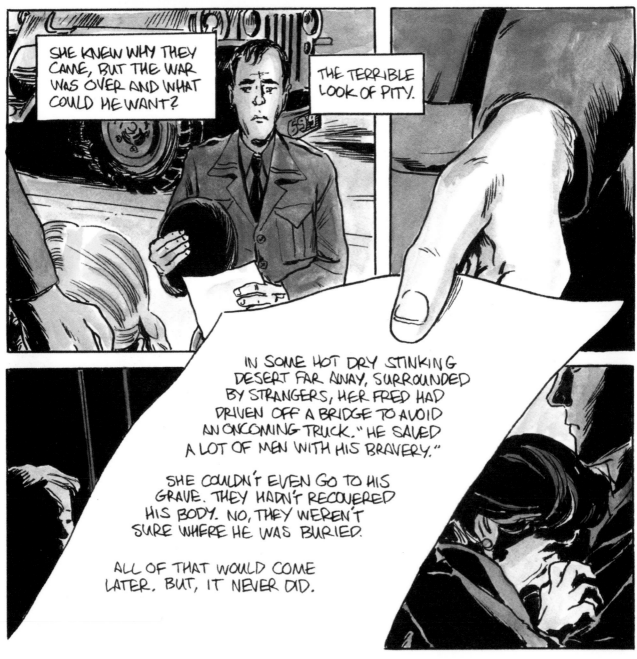

SHE KNEW WHY THEY CAME, BUT THE WAR WAS OVER AND WHAT COULD HE WANT?

THE TERRIBLE LOOK OF PITY.

IN SOME HOT DRY STINKING DESERT FAR AWAY, SURROUNDED BY STRANGERS, HER FRED HAD DRIVEN OFF A BRIDGE TO AVOID AN ONCOMING TRUCK. "HE SAVED A LOT OF MEN WITH HIS BRAVERY."

SHE COULDN'T EVEN GO TO HIS GRAVE. THEY HADN'T RECOVERED HIS BODY. NO, THEY WEREN'T SURE WHERE HE WAS BURIED.

ALL OF THAT WOULD COME LATER. BUT, IT NEVER DID.

THEN, THEY TRIED TO TAKE JUNE AWAY FROM HER.
THE RATIONALE OFFERED WAS THAT AS A SINGLE
WOMAN SHE WAS NOT ELIGIBLE TO ADOPT.
SHE HAD GIVEN HER HUSBAND, AND IN RETURN,
THEY TRIED TO TAKE HER CHILD.

HER LOWER LIP TOOK ON A THRUST OF HURT AND RESOLVE.

SO MUCH OF
HER ENERGY
WENT INTO
THE FIGHT
TO KEEP HER
DAUGHTER

BUT, SHE DID KEEP JUNE.

IT WAS HARD, BUT SHE WON.

ALL THAT CONNECTED HER TO HIM NOW WAS THE ACHE IN HER BODY.

THE SOLID OAK HEAD-BOARD OF HETTY'S BED SPARKLED, AS IF IT HAD BEEN VARNISHED WITH GLITTER.

BUT A CLOSER INSPECTION SHOWED THAT THE EFFECT CAME FROM TINY GLASS SHARDS, FROM WHEN HER WINDOW BLEW IN.

the outing

THE ROYAL INSIGNIA ON THE LONDON COURT PAPERS WITH ITS LONG PARTS AND PARTIES MADE EVERYTHING LOOK VERY IMPORTANT.

BUT THE INSIDE OF THE WHITE MARBLE BUILDING WITH ITS ENDLESS STAIRS AND CORRIDORS APPEARED STRANGELY DULL.

HAVE A SEAT.

THERE WAS SOMETHING IN THE RECEPTIONIST'S MOVEMENTS THAT RESEMBLED A SMALL BROWN RODENT.

HER TINY PLASTIC PEARLS LOOKED INCONGRUOUS WITH THE GRAVITY OF THE OCCASION.

BUT THEN, HETTY FELT SMALL TOO.

THE TICKING OF THE LARGE CLOCK ON THE WALL

SLOWED DOWN

TO A RUNNY THUMPING

PERHAPS IT WAS THE BLOOD IN HER EARS, OR HER HEART, OR MAYBE THE ROOM HAD FILLED WITH WATER AND SHE WAS MOVING ABOUT IN A WATERY WORLD.

AT THE VERY LEAST, HER SENSES WERE SWIMMING.

THEN FOR NO APPARENT REASON, THE PEARLS
SEEMED TO MOVE TOWARDS HER,
FLOATING THROUGH THE DIM LIGHT.

YOU MAY
GO IN NOW.

SHE WAS CAREFUL
NOT TO LEAVE HER
GLOVES OR HER BAG,
TOOK A QUICK HIDDEN
GLANCE AT HER SHOES
TO SEE THAT THEY
WERE SHINING.

"THE SHOES
MUST ALWAYS
BE POLISHED
FRONT AND BACK."

"...OR PEOPLE
WILL KNOW WHAT
SORT OF PERSON
YOU ARE."

A UNIFORMED MAN
USHERED HER INTO
A LONG CHAMBER

HE INDICATED THAT SHE
SIT IN THE CHAIR IN THE
CENTER OF THE ROOM.

BUT FAR AWAY AT THE OTHER END OF THE ROOM, A ROW OF CROWS SAT AT THE DESK BEFORE HER.

ONE'S EYES SHONE WILDLY WITH A JAUNDICED GLINT.

MRS. MARTIN.

...IS IT MRS. MARTIN?

IS THERE ANY CONFUSION?

THIS LAST WAS MEANT FOR HIS ASSOCIATES

I AM A WIDOW.

AH, WELL.... MRS. MARTIN.

WE ARE HERE TO DETERMINE THE BEST COURSE FOR LITTLE MARGUERITE.

AND, OF COURSE, FOR YOU.

SO I HOPE YOU WILL FEEL COMFORTABLE AS YOU ANSWER OUR QUESTIONS.

WE ASK ONLY TO GET TO THE HEART OF THE MATTER.

HE IMAGINED PULLING A WORM FROM THE GROUND, STANDING OVER IT AND JERKING OUT ITS UNWILLING BODY

SHORT HARD TUGS UNTIL IT WAS EXPOSED TO THE SUNLIGHT

HE SAW ITS PINK WRIGGLING NAKED BODY HANGING BEFORE HIM, AS IT WAS BURNED AND BLINDED BY THE SUNLIGHT.

SO LET ME BE CLEAR

THE WORLD WAS OFF-KILTER

SHE FELT AS THOUGH SHE HAD BEEN WALKING SIDEWAYS TO THE GROUND.

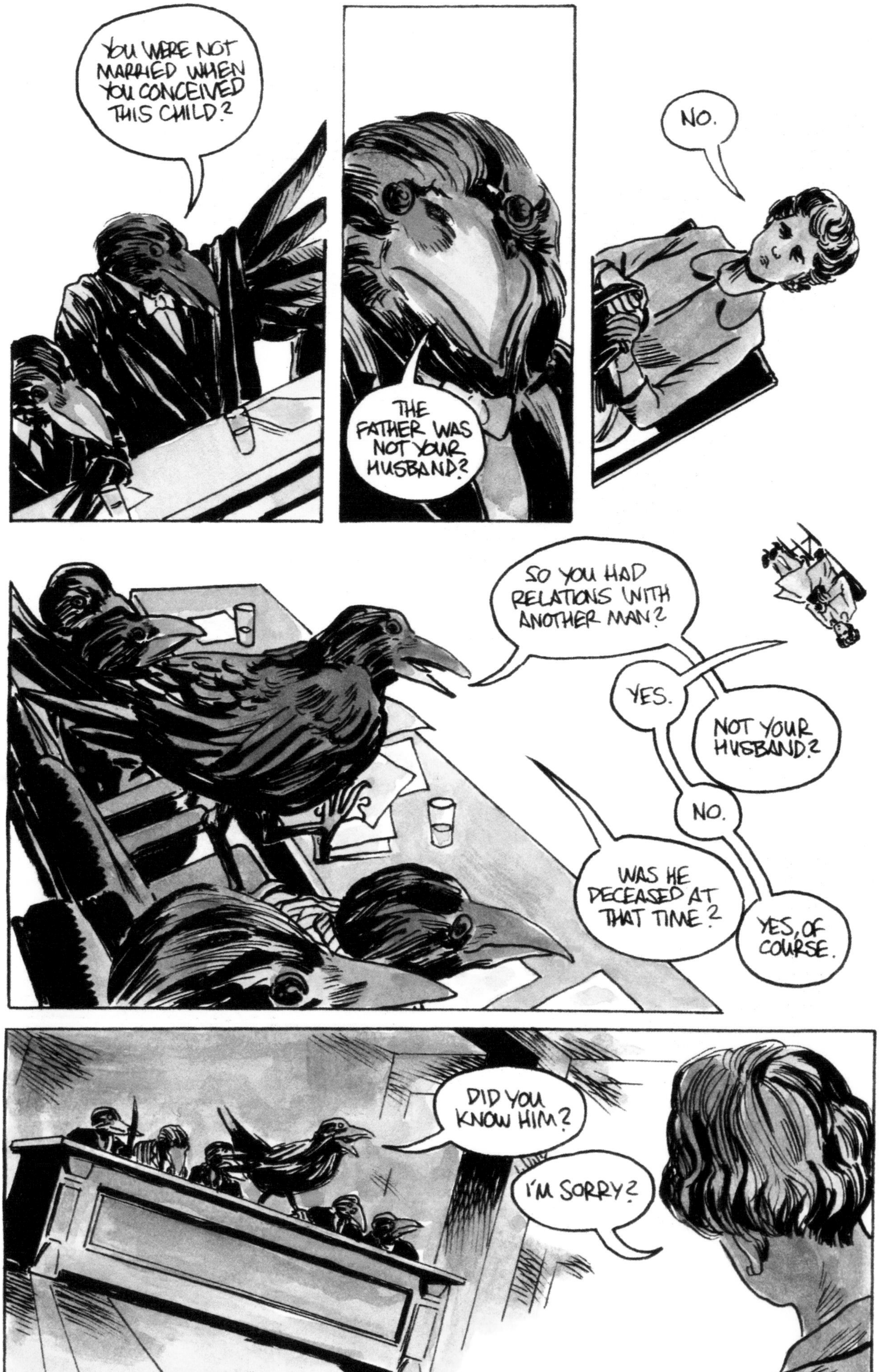
YOU WERE NOT MARRIED WHEN YOU CONCEIVED THIS CHILD?
THE FATHER WAS NOT YOUR HUSBAND?
NO.
SO YOU HAD RELATIONS WITH ANOTHER MAN?
YES.
NOT YOUR HUSBAND?
NO.
WAS HE DECEASED AT THAT TIME?
YES, OF COURSE.
DID YOU KNOW HIM?
I'M SORRY?

THE FLOCK RUSTLED ON THEIR PERCHES.

DID YOU KNOW THE FATHER OF THE CHILD OR NOT?

HE WAS STATIONED IN PORTSMOUTH DURING THE WAR AND BILLETED AT MY HOUSE.

SO YOU HAD KNOWN HIM WHILE YOUR HUSBAND WAS ALIVE?

THE BIRD FELT PLEASURE IN THE PULLING SENSATION

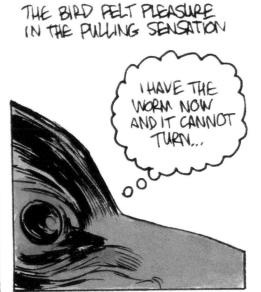

I HAVE THE WORM NOW AND IT CANNOT TURN...

HIS BIRD BRAIN STRAYED FOR A MINUTE AS HE PREENED HIMSELF.

HE INSPECTED THE CREATURE BEFORE HIM.

NOT VERY YOUNG, BUT VERY JUICY

HE COULD SMELL THE FEAR EMANATING FROM IT.

BUT THERE IS ANOTHER ONE SOMEWHERE

A TINY JUICY LITTLE PINKER ONE.

THE ROOM HAD BECOME
UNBEARABLY HOT AND
THE SWEAT WAS RUNNING
DOWN THE SIDES OF
HER BODY BENEATH
HER SUIT. SHE WORE
A GREY SUIT. IT WAS
VERY SMART.

BUT SHE DID NOT FEEL
SMART, SHE FELT SICK
AND DIRTY AND ON
THE BRINK OF TEARS.

TO CRY MIGHT PROVE
FATAL, BECAUSE
THEY MIGHT SEE THAT
SHE COULD NOT
CONTROL HERSELF.
THAT'S EXACTLY
WHAT THEY THOUGHT.

THEY WERE LOOKING
AT HER AND THINKING
ABOUT HER HAVING
SEX WITH A MAN,
ANY MAN, ANY MAN,
IN ANY PLACE, OF
ANY KIND, IT DIDN'T
MATTER.

THEIR FOCUS WAS ON HER, ENTIRELY ON HER. SEVEN PAIRS OF EYES ALL LOOKING AT HER AND THINKING ABOUT HER HAVING SEX.

SHE FELT UTTERLY NAKED AND ASHAMED. ASHAMED NOT BECAUSE OF WHAT SHE HAD DONE, ALTHOUGH GOD KNOWS, SHE WAS ASHAMED ABOUT THAT, BUT ASHAMED BY THE PALPABLE THOUGHTS THAT WERE FLOATING IN THE MUGGY AIR ABOVE THEM.

SHE COULDN'T WET HER LIPS TO SPEAK AND THE LACK OF AIR WAS MAKING HER MOUTH TASTE OF COTTON.

YES, HE WAS IN PORTSMOUTH, WHEN THE WAR WAS ON, AND THEN HE MORE OR LESS STAYED IN THE SOUTH WHEN THE WAR WAS OVER.

HE WAS NOT FROM THE SOUTH?

NO.

WHAT DO YOU MEAN, "MORE OR LESS"?

HE WENT HOME SEVERAL TIMES FOR A SHORT WHILE BUT CAME BACK.

AND WHY DIDN'T YOU MARRY?

THAT WOULD'VE SEEMED THE THING TO DO, NO?

HE WAS ALREADY MARRIED.

A MARRIED MAN?

YES.

WITH CHILDREN?

YES.

I SEE.

AND YOU KNEW OF HIS FAMILY?

YES.

DID IT NOT STRIKE YOU AS WRONG, MRS. MARTIN, TO HAVE RELATIONS WITH A MARRIED MAN?

ESPECIALLY SINCE HE HAD CHILDREN AND PRESUMABLY A WIFE WHO WERE DEPENDENT ON HIM?

YES, BUT...

THERE ARE NO BUTS, MRS. MARTIN. LET US EXAMINE YOUR STATE OF MIND.

KRAWK

IT LOOKED AT HER SHINY SHOES. IN GENERAL, IT LIKED SHINY THINGS.

THOSE BLACK SOFT LEATHER SHOES LOOKED LIKE DELICIOUS SLUGS.

SHE CERTAINLY IS A PLUMP ONE

I COULD PECK PECK PECK AWAY

AND VERY GOOD SHE'D BE, TOO.

THE OTHERS LOOKED AT HER FROM THE ONE SIDE AS IF THE SIGHT OF HER WAS TOO MUCH FOR THEM TO LOOK AT FULL ON.

HAVE YOU EVER BEEN HOSPITALIZED FOR A MENTAL CONDITION?

NO.

HAD ANY PROBLEMS IN THE AREA OF THAT SORT OF THING?

NO.

THERE'S NOTHING TO BE ASHAMED OF IF YOU ARE SUFFERING FROM MENTAL ILLNESS, YOU KNOW.

ARE YOU SURE YOU HAVE NEVER BEEN TREATED FOR MENTAL ILLNESS?

WELL, THE DOCTOR HAS GIVEN ME SOMETHING FOR MY NERVES.

ESPECIALLY AFTER I LOST MY HUSBAND.

THE BIRD AT THE FAR RIGHT BEGAN SCRATCHING AT SOMETHING ON THE TABLE.

ARE YOU ABLE TO READ AND WRITE?

YES

CHIC CKATE! CHIC

AT WHAT AGE DID YOU LEAVE SCHOOL?

HETTY COULDN'T SEE STRAIGHT.

THE ROOM BEGAN TO CLOSE IN AND EXPAND FROM ONE MOMENT TO THE NEXT.

FOURTEEN, LIKE EVERYONE ELSE.

DO YOU ATTEND CHURCH?

YES, WELL, NOT EVERY WEEK.

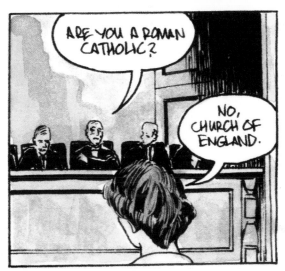

ARE YOU A ROMAN CATHOLIC?

NO, CHURCH OF ENGLAND.

DO YOU DRINK, MRS. MARTIN?

GOOD HEAVENS, NO.

A SIMPLE NO WILL DO... THANK YOU.

ANY HISTORY OF PROSTITUTION?

NO.

NO ARRESTS OF ANY KIND?

NO.

MORE SCRATCHING FROM THE BIRD AT THE FAR RIGHT.

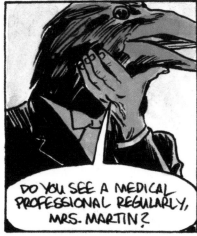

YES.

VERY WELL THEN.

I WILL NOT ASK YOU FOR AN EXPLANATION, BECAUSE THERE IS NO REAL EXPLANATION FOR THIS SITUATION. YOU DO NOT APPEAR TO BE MENTALLY UNBALANCED. YOU ARE NOT A DRUNK OR A PROSTITUTE. THIS SITUATION IS QUITE UNFATHOMABLE TO THE COURT. YOU ARE A WOMAN OF APPARENT GOOD STANDING AND WE SEE FURTHER THAT YOU HAVE AN ADOPTED DAUGHTER ALREADY.

DOES IT NOT MAKE YOU CONCERNED ABOUT THE SHAME THAT YOU BRING ON THIS OTHER INNOCENT CHILD?

WHAT ABOUT YOUR PARENTS?

TO BRING AN ILLEGITIMATE CHILD INTO THE WORLD, TO SHAME HER AND THEM, AND WHEN YOU ARE ALONE...

AND NOW PRESUMABLY WILL HAVE NO MEANS OF SUPPORT.

I HAVE A HOUSE.

I SEE.

THIS IS VERY DIFFICULT, MRS. MARTIN.

HOW DO YOU INTEND TO KEEP THE CHILD?

THE COURT SEES YOU HAVE NO VISIBLE MEANS OF SUPPORT.

WILL YOU NOW ATTEMPT TO CLAIM BENEFITS?

DO YOU THINK YOU ARE A FIT MOTHER?

DO YOU REASONABLY THINK THAT YOU ARE SOUND AND MORALLY ABLE TO TAKE CARE OF THESE CHILDREN?

WOULD IT NOT BE BETTER IF THE CHILD WERE PUT INTO A HOME, PUT UP FOR ADOPTION?

NO, I WANT TO KEEP MY DAUGHTER.

I BEG YOUR PARDON?

I WANT TO KEEP MY DAUGHTER, AND I RENT OUT ROOMS AT MY HOUSE FOR MONEY.

IF I NEED TO, I CAN WORK.

WORK? WORK? TAKING IN LODGERS? ISN'T THAT WHAT GOT US INTO THIS DREADFUL STATE OF AFFAIRS?

I WANT TO KEEP MY BABY.

AND I KNOW I CAN TAKE CARE OF HER.

DO YOU INTEND FOR YOUR CHILD TO HAVE THE PROPER MORAL INSTRUCTION?

PERHAPS FROM YOUR VICAR?

HE IS AWARE OF YOUR STATE, ISN'T HE?

YOU HAVE CHRISTENED THE CHILD, HAVEN'T YOU?

OF COURSE. THAT IS...

I WILL HAVE HER CHRISTENED.

AND SHE CAN GO TO SUNDAY SCHOOL

AH YES

VERY SOUND.

THE BIRD THOUGHT OF THE FONT AND HOW HE COULD DRINK FROM ITS EVERLASTING WATERS.

THANK YOU, MRS. MARTIN. PLEASE WAIT OUTSIDE.

BACK IN THE SEAT SHE HAD PREVIOUSLY OCCUPIED, HETTY COULD HEAR SOME KIND OF UPROAR BEHIND THE DOOR, AND THEN EVERYTHING WENT QUIET.

THE CLOCK DRAGGED ITS ARMS ACROSS THE FACE

FIVE MINUTES BECAME TWENTY, AND THE WAVES OF NAUSEA GREW IN STRENGTH.

THEY WILL NOTIFY YOU BY MAIL.

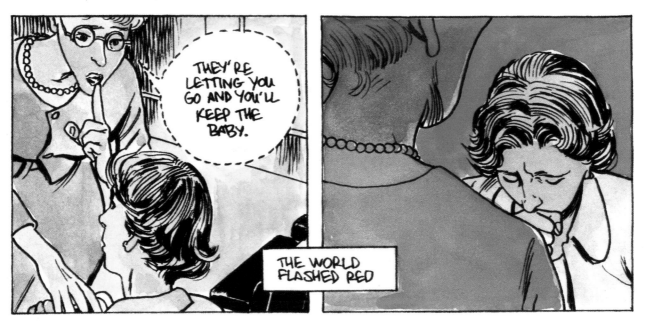

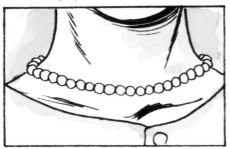

A HUNDRED MILES AWAY, A BABY AND A TWELVE-YEAR-OLD GIRL WAITED WITH A GOOD NEIGHBOR.

WHEN PEOPLE WERE NOT LOOKING, HETTY CRIED ON THE WAY HOME. SHE HAD CRIED SO OFTEN, TEARS CAME LIKE OLD FRIENDS. SO MUCH OF HER LIFE HAD TO BE CONDUCTED IN THE SHADOWS NOW. EVEN THOUGH THE NEWS WAS GOOD, SHE FELT AS THOUGH THE GROUND UNDER HER FEET WAS GONE. AS THE TRAIN PULLED INTO PORTSMOUTH STATION, SHE WAS SPENT. BUT THEN, SHE WAS ALWAYS ON THE EDGE NOW.

NOW THAT EVERYONE KNEW.

AS THE DRY DOCKS DRAINED, SHE COULD HEAR THE BARKING OF THE STRANDED EELS. THE DOCKMEN WOULD KILL THEM IF THEY COULD.

THE SEAGULLS CIRCLED AND SCREAMED...

SQUABBLING OVER THE CLAMS AT LOW TIDE.

GREEDY FOR THE PASSENGERS' DISCARDED SANDWICHES, THEY RAN CLOSE TO HETTY'S FEET...

BEFORE FLYING UP TO WATCH FROM THE DREARY GREY SKY.

ARRETON DOWNS

MOTHER HAD WARNED ME NOT TO STARE WHEN I MET HER, BUT MRS. ORCHARD HAD LONG SINCE GIVEN UP WORRYING ABOUT HER MOUSTACHE, AS INDEED SHE SHOULD HAVE.

HER LARGE FRAME ECHOED THE SHOULDERS OF THE HILLS OF THE ISLE OF WIGHT.

I DID NOT CLOSE MY 8-YEAR-OLD MOUTH FOR THE ENTIRE TIME MUMMY WAS CHATTING.

SHE WAS HELPFUL IN DIRECTING US TO THE EVERYDAY DETAILS OF VILLAGE LIFE.

SHE WAS A SENSIBLE WOMAN, NOT UNFRIENDLY, NOR OVERLY.

THAT'S WHERE YOU'LL BE FINDING FRESH MILK AND EGGS.

WHEN SHE WENT ON HER WAY, WE TURNED TO VISIT ANCIENT MR. CHIVERTON.

HE WAS A TENANT OF ONE OF THE WEE 17th-CENTURY COTTAGES OF WHICH MY STEPFATHER, "UNCLE" BERT WAS NOW THE LANDLORD.

THE EARLY BEANS' FRESH SMELL ESCAPED ACROSS THE GARDEN AS MR. CHIVERTON SNAPPED A FEW STEMS.

HIS CHEEKS SHONE LIKE POLISHED APPLES.

DESPITE HIS YEARS, HE STILL GOT ABOUT AND WAS DELIGHTED TO SEE US.

HELLO, MY DEAR HETTY.

AND YOU MUST BE LITTLE MARGUERITE.

FANCY A CUP OF TEA?

IF IT'S NOT TOO MUCH TROUBLE... I DON'T WANT TO PUT YOU TO ANY BOTHER.

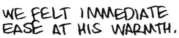
WE FELT IMMEDIATE EASE AT HIS WARMTH.

TICK

MOIND YOUR 'EADS.

HIS WAY OF SPEAKING WAS COUNTRY, BUT HE HAD A DELICACY TO HIM.

WE WERE HAPPY TO HAVE TEA WITH HIM.

INSIDE, COOL EMANATED FROM CHALKY WALLS THAT HELD THE DAMP YEAR-ROUND.

MR. CHIVERTON KEPT A FIRE GOING THROUGH ALL THE SEASONS.

THE COTTAGES HAD NO HOT WATER, AND NO INDOOR BATH ROOM, FOR THAT MATTER.

FOR BATHING, WATER WAS HEATED ON THE FIRE.

I GUESSED THAT HE MUST USE THE METAL TUB TO HAVE A BATH ONCE IN A WHILE, THOUGH IT WASN'T SOMETHING THAT WAS DISCUSSED IN FRONT OF ME.

BUT FOR ALL OF THE INCONVENIENCES THAT MIGHT HAVE BOTHERED THE ADULT WORLD, I MIGHT AS WELL HAVE BEEN IN FAIRYLAND.

EVERYTHING IN THE ROOM WAS FREE OF DUST.
IT WAS ALL BRIGHT AND SHINY LIKE HIM.

WOULD YOU LIKE A NICE CUP O' MILK?

I SAT UP STRAIGHT IN MY CHAIR AND TRIED TO MIND MY MANNERS.

YES, PLEASE.

THEY TALKED ABOUT THIS AND THAT, OF THINGS THAT HOLD NO INTEREST TO A CHILD AND ARE NOT MEANT TO.

I SUPPOSE THEY TALKED OF LEAKS AND FAUCETS, GUTTERS AND ALL THE THINGS THAT AFFECT LIVES, PARTICULARLY IN THE COUNTRY.

BUT WHEN THEY BEGAN TO TALK ABOUT MOTHER'S PLANS FOR HER NEW GARDEN, AND A GARDEN SHE HAD HAD AS A LITTLE GIRL...

...I COULD NOT HELP BUT LISTEN IN WONDER. SHE SPOKE OF LARKSPUR AND PANSIES, WALLFLOWERS FOR THEIR SCENT.

ROSES AND SWEET PEAS.

CHAMOMILE, RUE, ROSEMARY, DAISIES, AND MARGUERITES (MY NAMESAKE)

HERBS THAT DO YOU GOOD AND THINGS YOU SHOULD WATCH OUT FOR.

MR. CHIVERTON TALKED OF THINGS THAT ARE GOOD FOR A COLD AND THINGS THAT ARE GOOD FOR A BACKACHE.

MOTHER POINTED OUT THAT FOXGLOVES WERE THE SOURCE OF DIGITALIS, WHICH HAD SAVED HER SISTER'S LIFE FOR QUITE A FEW YEARS.

I REMEMBERED LILIES OF THE VALLEY BECAUSE GRANDMA TOLD ME THAT THE FAIRIES LIKE TO HIDE UNDER THEIR LEAVES.

SHE HAD THEM IN PROFUSION AT THE END OF HER GARDEN

BUT HOW DID MY MOTHER KNOW THIS?

I HAD ALWAYS THOUGHT THAT GRANNY AND I WERE THE ONLY ONES TO SHARE THESE THINGS.

PERHAPS THE COUNTRYSIDE BROUGHT OUT ANOTHER PART OF HER.

AS THE LAST OF THE SECOND POT OF TEA WAS DRAINED, WE ROSE TO LEAVE. MR. CHIVERTON PROMISED MOTHER CUTTINGS WHEN SHE WAS READY TO HAVE THEM.

HE TOOK US TO THE END OF HIS GARDEN WHERE THE STREAM RAN AND ADJOINED OUR LOT.

YOU'LL FIND ALL KINDS OF FROGS AND WHATNOT IN THERE.

VERY GOOD WORTER THAT IS.

THAT'S THE WORTER THAT FILLS THE WELL, FILTERS THROUGH ALL THE DOWNS

AND COMES OUT CLEAN AS A WHISTLE.

CAN I PADDLE MY FEET?

YOU'LL HAVE TA ARSK YOUR MOTHER, MY DEAR.

AND I KNEW THAT THE PROBABLE ANSWER WOULD BE NO. EVEN THOUGH I WAS RIGHT, I WASN'T DISAPPOINTED FOR LONG.

THE SIGHTS AND SOUNDS OF THE PLACE QUICKLY TOOK COMMAND OF MY IMAGINATION.

THE COTTAGES FACED A FIELD THAT SPREAD FLAT IN ALL DIRECTIONS AS FAR AS ONE COULD SEE.

ON IT, A BIRD WAR RAGED.

CROWS GUARDED THE FIELD FROM THE NOISY CHALLENGE OF THE SEAGULLS.

IT APPEARED A NO-MAN'S-LAND TO MY EYES.

PART OF THE NEW HOLDINGS WAS A LARGE STRETCH OF LAND AT THE END OF WHICH BERT HAD INSTALLED A MOBILE HOME.

THE SYNTHETIC GREEN STRUCTURE ON THE GREY CEMENT BLOCK WAS THE REAL WORLD. IT HAD INVOLVED PLANNING PERMISSION AND LOCAL COUNCILS AND OTHER THINGS THAT I CARED NOTHING ABOUT.

IT WAS TO BE A RETREAT UNTIL WE HAD ACCESS TO THE LARGER COTTAGE.

THIS WOULD HAPPEN WHEN THE ELDERLY PEOPLE WHO LIVED THERE MOVED INTO THE FULLY PLUMBED MODERN HOUSE THAT THE AUTHORITIES WERE BUILDING FOR THEM HALF A MILE AWAY.

OR, WHAT SEEMED EQUALLY PLAUSIBLE TO ME WITH THE BRUTAL PRAGMATISM OF CHILDHOOD, UNTIL THEY DIED.

THEY DIDN'T TAKE CARE OF THEIR GARDEN AND THEY WEREN'T VERY SOCIABLE.

SO I SPENT VERY LITTLE TIME THINKING ABOUT THEM,

AND I FORBADE MYSELF TO ANTICIPATE THE ENCHANTED DAY WHEN WE COULD MOVE INTO THE HOUSE

ON SUNDAY NIGHTS WE HEADED ON THE BUS, ON THE FERRY, BACK TO PORTSMOUTH.

LIFE WENT ON UNTIL THE FOLLOWING WEEK'S END, WHEN BAGS WERE PACKED AGAIN.

JUST A FEW BITS AND PIECES WE'LL NEED.

I PUT IN SOME NICE BACON

AND WE CAN JUST MAKE DO WITH A HAM SALAD FOR DINNER.

AND SO IT WENT, ALL THROUGH THE SUMMER.

I HATED THE LONG WAITS, BUT I LOVED TO BE IN THE COUNTRY.

THE DOWNS ARE RENOWNED FOR THEIR BEAUTY.

FROM ON HIGH THE FIELDS SLOPE DOWN, INTERRUPTED BY SMALL CHALK CLIFFS, LIKE A GIANT'S BED QUILT, WITH HEDGEROWS AND SMALL WOODS STITCHING ALONG THE PATCHES.

BUT, MOTHER DIDN'T SEEM TO BE MAKING ANY START ON THE PROMISED GARDEN, AND I COULDN'T WAIT TO DIG AND PLANT AND JUST BE PART OF THE COUNTRY LIFE.

IT ALWAYS SEEMED THAT SHE WAS TOO TIRED, AND SHE **WAS**...

HAVING WORKED A LONG WEEK, AND BERT ALWAYS WANTED HER COMPANY, AND I WAS GENERALLY LEFT TO MY OWN DEVICES.

MOTHER HAD HAD ME WHEN SHE WAS FORTY. I WAS A LATE CHILD. BERT WAS TEN YEARS HER SENIOR AND SO ALREADY OLD.

MOTHER SAID OLDER PARENTS PROVIDE A MORE CALMING INTELLECTUAL ENVIRONMENT. YOUNGER PARENTS WERE LIABLE TO GET OUT AND RUN AROUND MORE.

AND ALTHOUGH I THOUGHT THERE WAS SOMETHING OF AN EXCUSE IN HER REASONING, I LOVED MY MOTHER AND TRIED NOT TO BE A NUISANCE.

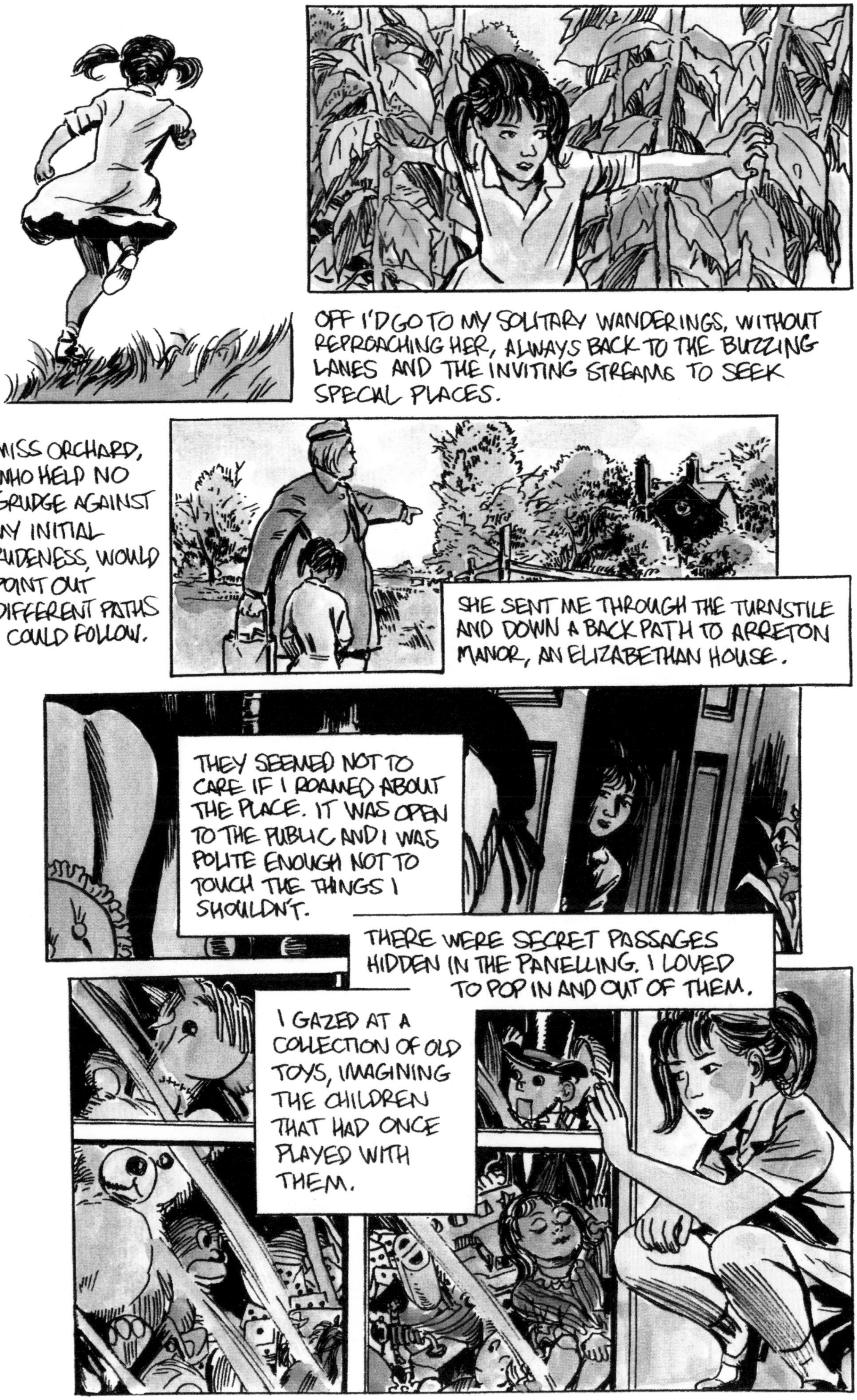
OFF I'D GO TO MY SOLITARY WANDERINGS, WITHOUT REPROACHING HER, ALWAYS BACK TO THE BUZZING LANES AND THE INVITING STREAMS TO SEEK SPECIAL PLACES.
MISS ORCHARD, WHO HELD NO GRUDGE AGAINST MY INITIAL RUDENESS, WOULD POINT OUT DIFFERENT PATHS I COULD FOLLOW.
SHE SENT ME THROUGH THE TURNSTILE AND DOWN A BACK PATH TO ARRETON MANOR, AN ELIZABETHAN HOUSE.
THEY SEEMED NOT TO CARE IF I ROAMED ABOUT THE PLACE. IT WAS OPEN TO THE PUBLIC AND I WAS POLITE ENOUGH NOT TO TOUCH THE THINGS I SHOULDN'T.
THERE WERE SECRET PASSAGES HIDDEN IN THE PANELLING. I LOVED TO POP IN AND OUT OF THEM.
I GAZED AT A COLLECTION OF OLD TOYS, IMAGINING THE CHILDREN THAT HAD ONCE PLAYED WITH THEM.

I VISITED THE WALLED GARDEN AND FANTASIZED THAT I MIGHT FIND MY OWN SECRET GARDEN, OR ANY GARDEN, FOR THAT MATTER.

I MADE UP LITTLE DANCES ON THE LAWNS AND NEAR THE ROSE GARDENS AND IMAGINED MYSELF TO BE VERY SPECIAL.

THE OLD GRAVEYARD NEXT TO THE ANGLICAN CHURCH MADE ME LONG TO KNOW THE PEOPLE WHO LAY UNDER THE OLD STONES. I SPOKE TO THEM ALOUD AND SHARED MY SECRETS. SOMETIMES I PUT DAISIES AND BUTTERCUPS ON THE HEADSTONES.

BUT NOTHING EVER STIRRED

AND NO ONE EVER SPOKE BACK.

THE WORLD ALL SEEMED PERFECTLY ORDERED AND KEMPT AND IT WAS ALL GOING ALONG AND IT SEEMED LIKE IT DIDN'T WANT MY HELP.

66

EVERYTHING WAS ALREADY DONE.

I ONLY WANTED TO BE PART OF SOMETHING.

THE FARMS, THE CHICKEN RAISING, THE VEGETABLE GROWING, OR PERHAPS TO HELP WITH THE TEA ROOM IN THE BACK OF THE MANOR...

WHERE PEOPLE CAME AND WENT LIKE CLOCKWORK AND TABLES WERE LAID AND CLEARED WITH PERFECT PRECISION.

THE FIELDS WERE ALL PLOUGHED IN STRAIGHT ROWS AND PLANTED WITH NEAT LINES OF GREEN.

"STAY OUT OF THE WAY" WAS THE ADULT MANTRA.

I ASKED IF I COULD CLEAR OUT THE OLD SHED TO MAKE A CLUB HOUSE. NO ONE OBJECTED AND I WENT OFF, FINALLY WITH A TASK AND A PLACE TO BE.

I BEGAN TO SHOVEL LEAVES INTO A SACK.

THE SHOVEL WAS HEAVY, AND IT WAS HARD WORK.

I BORROWED A SHOVEL FROM THE OLD COUPLE.

THE SHED WAS CLOSER TO THEIR HOUSE THAN OUR MOBILE HOME, AND SO I BEGAN WITH SOLITARY DETERMINATION.

IT DID NOT SEEM AN IMPROBABLE TASK, AND EXCAVATING ALSO MIGHT YIELD FORGOTTEN TREASURE.

IF IT WORKED OUT, THE PLACE WOULD BE MINE.

WHEN MY MOTHER LOOKED IN ON ME, I WAS FILTHY AND COVERED WITH THE DUST OF DRY LEAVES.

AS I BRUSHED THE SWEAT AWAY, IT MADE MUD OF THE DIRT AND SCRATCHED MY SKIN.

I WAS DETERMINED TO SHOW NO SIGN OF WEAKNESS.

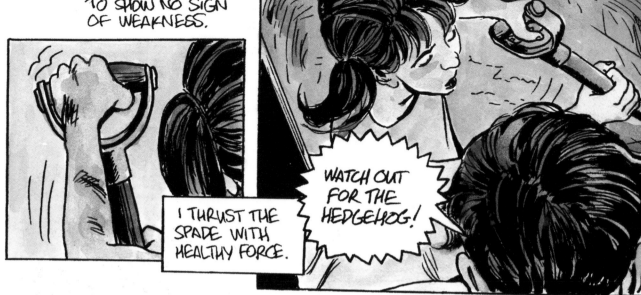

I THRUST THE SPADE WITH HEALTHY FORCE.

WATCH OUT FOR THE HEDGEHOG!

MAYBE IT HAS BABIES THERE TOO

AND THAT WAS THE END OF IT FOR ME. TEARS BEGAN TO FLOW AND A TERRIBLE SADNESS TOOK ME.

WAAAA

I DIDN'T BELONG THERE AND NOW I KNEW IT FOR SURE

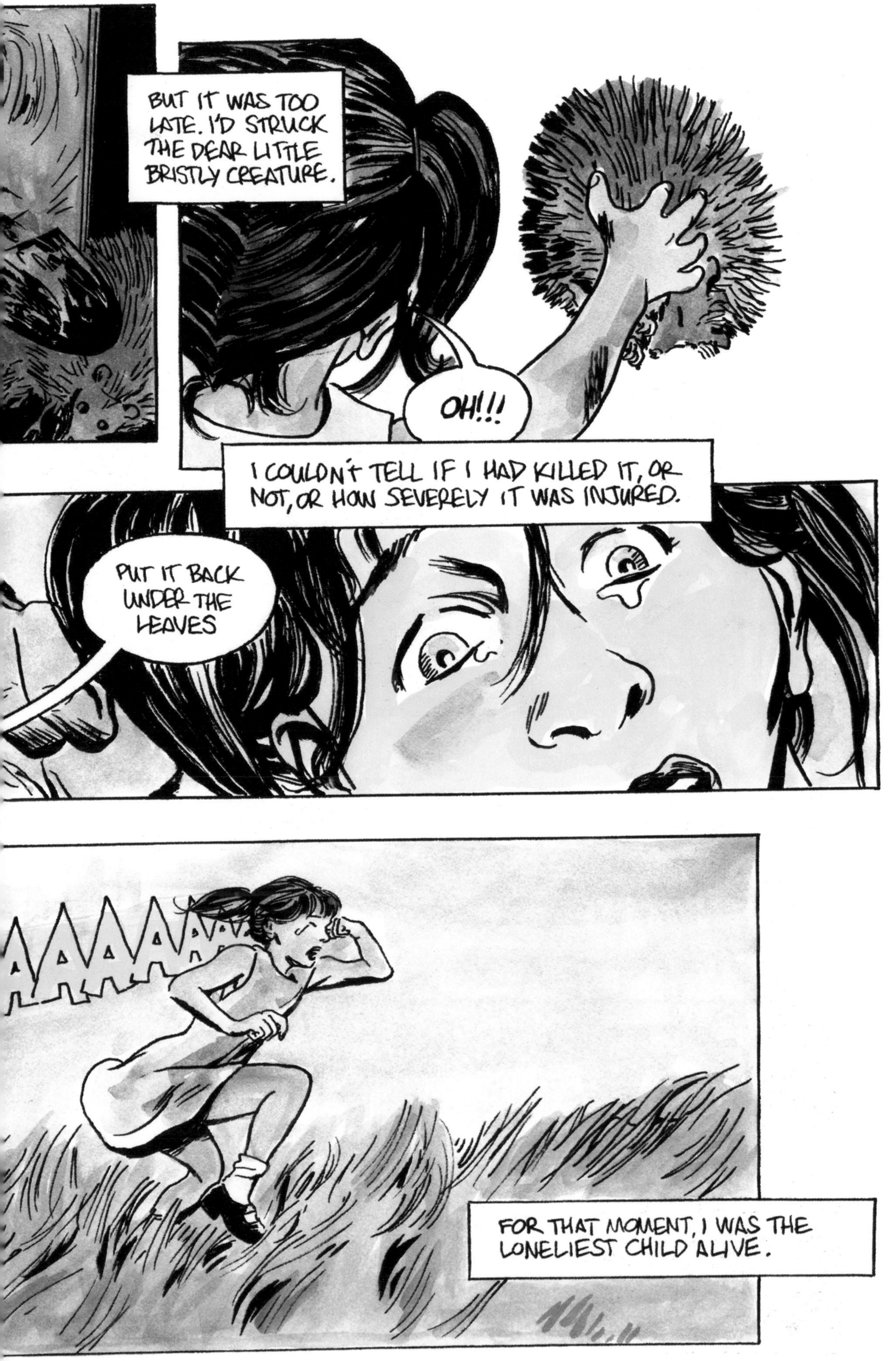
BUT IT WAS TOO LATE. I'D STRUCK THE DEAR LITTLE BRISTLY CREATURE.
OH!!!
I COULDN'T TELL IF I HAD KILLED IT, OR NOT, OR HOW SEVERELY IT WAS INJURED.
PUT IT BACK UNDER THE LEAVES
AAAAAA
FOR THAT MOMENT, I WAS THE LONELIEST CHILD ALIVE.

BUT IN THE WAY THE VERY YOUNG DO, SOON I BEGAN TO THINK OF NEW PLANS AND THE ADVENTURES THAT LAY BEFORE ME. I SURMISED THAT I COULDN'T HAVE DONE SO MUCH DAMAGE AND THAT THINGS MIGHT RIGHT THEMSELVES AFTER ALL.

MISS ORCHARD SEEMED NOT TO NOTICE ME.

I STOPPED TO WASH UP AT THE STREAM,

I'LL PICK SOME FLOWERS FOR MUM...

THE BLACK ON MY SHIRT WAS A SMUDGED REMINDER OF MY PRETEND TOUGHNESS.

I PICKED THE BLACKBERRIES AS I WENT.

BUT THE SPIKES CAUGHT ON MY CLOTHES AND DREW A FEW SPECKS OF BLOOD.

OW!

THE CHALK DOWN HAD WORN THROUGH THE GREEN OF THE GIANT'S SWEATER,

LOWER DOWN WERE THE ANCIENT BARROW MOUNDS OF THE NEOLITHIC PEOPLES.

LEGEND HAS IT THAT THEY ARE THE HALL OF THE LITTLE FOLK, WHO LIVE HIDDEN DEEP WITHIN.

THE NEARBY MANOR CHURCH TRACED ITSELF BACK TO THE 11th CENTURY AND EVEN BEFORE. I KNEW THAT FROM PEERING INTO GLASS CASES IN THE VESTRY. NOTHING MUCH HAD CHANGED HERE FOR A THOUSAND YEARS AT LEAST.

THE FIELDS, WHICH SEEMED CLOSE FROM A DISTANCE, MELTED AWAY.

AS THE YELLOW OF THE HAY RAN AWAY BEHIND ME.

THE TOP OF MY HEAD AND MY FACE FELT THE FULL FORCE OF THE SUN.

THEY THRONGED THE TREES THAT GREW BEHIND THE SWEET-SMELLING WILD ROSES.

UP AND UP I MARCHED. MY LEGS ACHED WITH THE UPHILL THRUST.

THE TRACTOR THAT HAD DRIVEN ALONG HERE ON A RAINY DAY LEFT GROOVES IN THE MUD, WHICH HAD DRIED IN DEEP RIDGES THAT MADE IT HARD TO KEEP MY FOOTING.

74

IN THE STUBBLE OF THE CROPPED WHEAT, THE SMALL BIRDS WENT ABOUT THEIR BUSINESS AS IF I WASN'T THERE.

AS THE FIELDS SEEMED TO LENGTHEN, SO THE BIRDS SEEMED TO MULTIPLY IN NUMBERS AND IN VARIETY.

I NEVER KNEW THE WORLD WAS SO ALIVE.

FIELD MICE CLIMBED UP THE FEW STRAGGLING EARS OF WHEAT THAT THE FARMERS HAD MISSED.

THEY HUNG UPSIDE-DOWN, IN DEFIANCE OF GRAVITY.

NOW THEY RAN, SWARMING ALL THROUGH THE UNDERGROWTH.

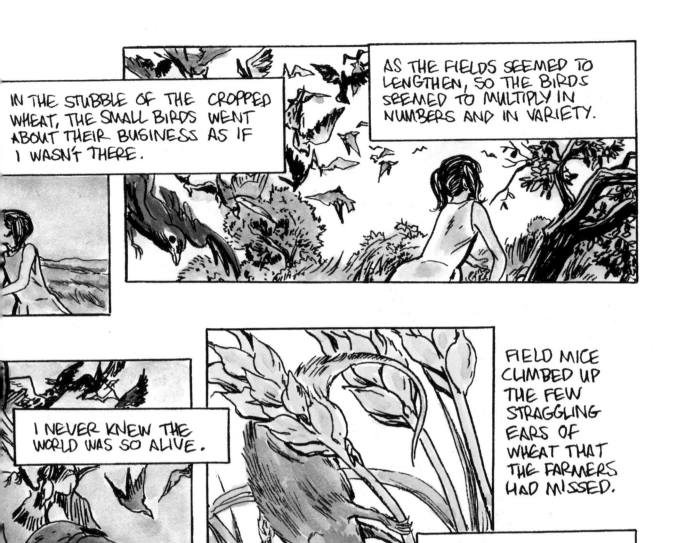

IN SOME PLACES THE PATH WAS BLOCKED AND I HAD TO DIVERT TO OTHER PATHS PARALLEL TO THE SUMMIT, TO COME TO THE NEXT PASSABLE GATE.

YET I WAS ENTHRALLED BY THIS SECRET WORLD AND DRAWN EVER UP AND OUT.

THE SUN ANGLED ACROSS THE COPSE.

BIRDS SWARMED THE WILD GARLIC FLOWERS.

75

THEY IN TURN MADE WAY FOR LITTLE WASPY CREATURES THAT WERE STATIONED ON EVERY BLOSSOM.

THE ROSES HOSTED GIANT BEES.

NOW IT WAS AS THOUGH I WERE ONE WITH THE PLACE.

AS IF I COULD UNDERSTAND THE RURAL CONVERSATION.

NEAR THE STREAMLET, VEILS OF GNATS THICKENED THE AIR.

THE SUN WAS MORE BRUTAL HERE. THE SHINY STALKS REFLECTED THE HEAT BACK AT ME.

PURPLE SUN SPOTS BEFORE MY EYES.

I DECIDED TO STRIKE OUT INTO THE FIELD, TO CROSS DIAGONALLY UP.

LARGE WELTS WERE COMING UP. IT PASSED TOLERANCE AND ENTERED MISERY.

AND BUTTERFLIES VIED TO ALIGHT ON THE BUTTERCUPS.

AS SHADOWS CROSSED, THE CRICKETS SANG A LAST CHORUS IN THE GRASSES WHERE THE STREAM RUSHED DOWNWARD.

I HAD GONE SEVERAL DIFFICULT MILES BEFORE I TURNED TO LOOK BACK.

FROM HERE, THE COTTAGES LOOKED LIKE SMALL WHITE HENS.

THE MOBILE HOME WAS COMPLETELY CAMOUFLAGED FROM VIEW.

I HAD TO SQUINT TO MOVE FORWARD.

THE CUT WHEAT STEMS SCRATCHED MY SKIN AS I WENT. AT FIRST IT WAS JUST A LITTLE SORE.

BUT SOON IT BECAME UNDENIABLY PAINFUL.

TURNING TO LOOK BACK, THE VASTNESS OF SPACE STRUCK ME.

THE WORLD SPRAWLED AWAY IN EVERY DIRECTION. NO SHADE, NO REFUGE.

JUST THE SEARING OF THE SUN AND ACRES OF BRUTAL STEMS.

EVERYTHING RUSHED AT ME. NATURE STOPPED HER BUSINESS AND A MILLION EYES TURNED TO LOOK AT ME.

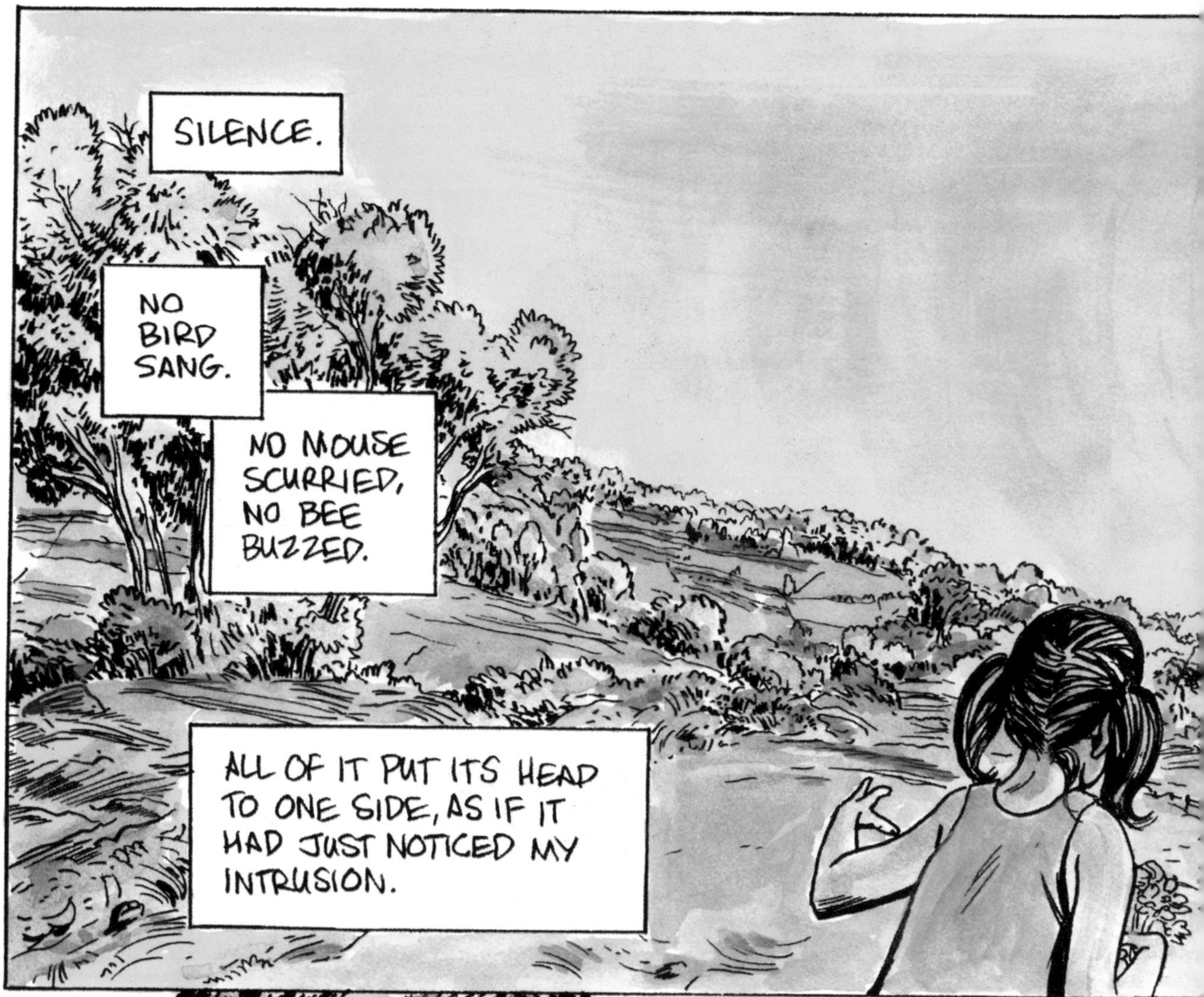
SILENCE.
NO BIRD SANG.
NO MOUSE SCURRIED, NO BEE BUZZED.
ALL OF IT PUT ITS HEAD TO ONE SIDE, AS IF IT HAD JUST NOTICED MY INTRUSION.

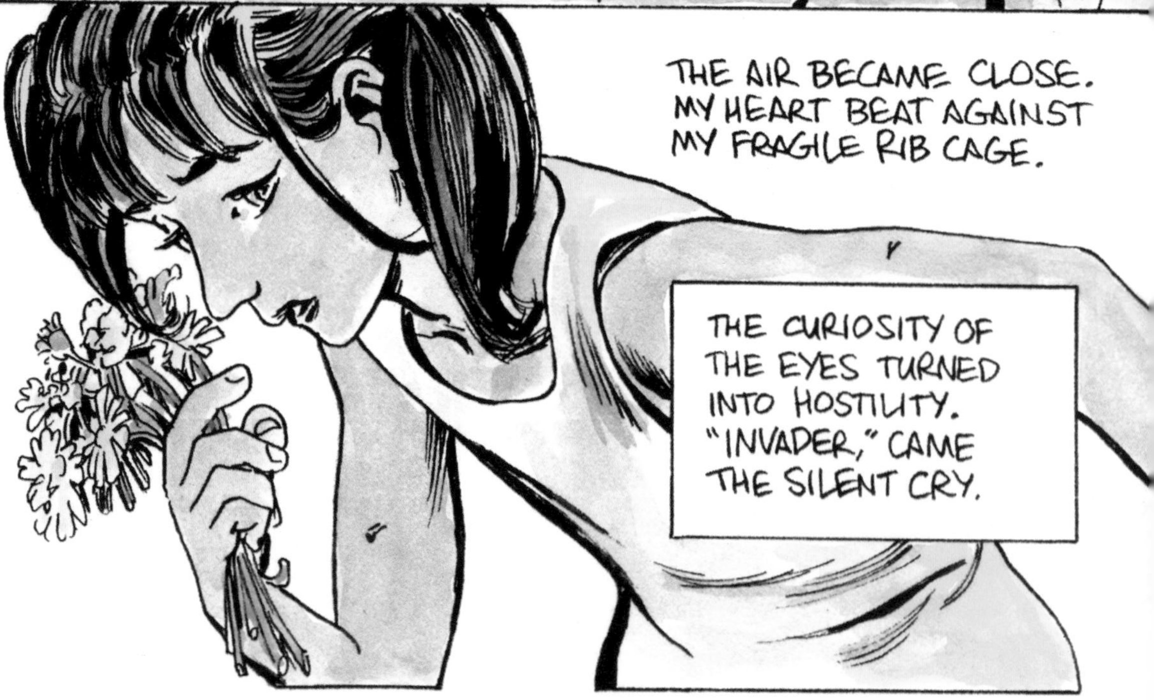
THE AIR BECAME CLOSE. MY HEART BEAT AGAINST MY FRAGILE RIB CAGE.
THE CURIOSITY OF THE EYES TURNED INTO HOSTILITY. "INVADER," CAME THE SILENT CRY.

FEAR SWEPT THROUGH ME. I WAS ALONE, MILES FROM ANYONE, ANYWHERE. METALLIC SALIVA CAME BITTER TO MY TONGUE. MY LUNGS REFUSED TO GIVE ME AIR. NATURE WAS NOT SWEETLY MAGIC, IT WAS WILD. THIS ENGLISH FIELD HELD A HIDDEN POTENCY. THE SKIES SPUN ABOVE ME AND THE FIELDS UNDULATED.

NEVER HAVE I FELT SO SMALL, NOT BEFORE, NOT NOW. THAT INSTANT STOLE MY IDENTITY AND EVERYTHING I THOUGHT I KNEW ABOUT LIFE, ABOUT MY PLACE IN THE WORLD.

PRESENTLY, HAVING WARNED ME, THE EYES TURNED AWAY AND THE WORLD RESUMED.

NATURE HAD CHECKED ME, TOO.

I BEGAN THE DESCENT, PAINFULLY PICKING MY WAY THROUGH.

THE SOIL SIGHED AND THE GROUND RELAXED BENEATH MY FEET.

" LESSON LEARNED, LITTLE GIRL."

"NOW YOU KNOW."

THE FIERY SKY CHASED ME HOME.

NOW I RAN

THE CLOUDS KEPT PACE ABOVE ME.

I FLEW OVER THE STILE AS THE EVENING BEGAN TO DRAIN INTO NIGHT.

MR. CHIVERTON WAS GATHERING A FEW EARLY BRUSSELS SPROUTS.

HAD QUITE A DAY, HAVEN'T YOU?

MMM

YAS, YOU'RE A LATE CHILD.

AT LEAST, THAT'S WHAT I THOUGHT HE SAID.

YOU HAS TO WATCH OUT UP THERE

HE DIDN'T QUALIFY THE COMMENT, BUT MOTIONED ME THROUGH THE GATE.

I'VE GOT SOMETHING FOR YOU.

JUST A MINUTE

THE TWILIGHT STARS GAVE THE WORLD A LUMINOUS HUE.

THE FLOWERS SPARKLED WITH A BRIGHTER RADIANCE.

I STOOD 80 POUNDS OF WONDER, AS FRAIL AND SWEET AS ANY FLOWER THERE.

HERE YAR THEN

YOW'LL LIKE THIS.

THIS BELONGED TO MY SISTER'S GIRL, IT DID.

IT WAS A LOCKET FILLED WITH DRIED LAVENDER AND TINY ROSE PETALS.

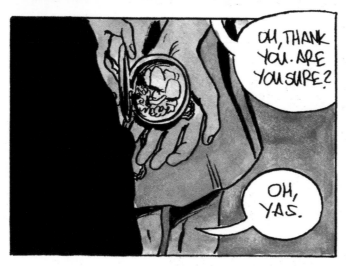

OH, THANK YOU. ARE YOU SURE?

OH, YAS.

I'M VERY SURE. NOW OFF YOU GO OR YOUR MUTHER 'ULL WORRY.

AS I WENT ALONG THE MAIN ROAD, I THOUGHT I SAW MISS ORCHARD IN THE CORNFIELD...

STANDING OUT IN THE BLUE VELVET.

FOR A SECOND, I PUZZLED OVER WHAT SHE WAS DOING.

BUT I COULD SEE MY MOTHER IN THE KITCHEN BAY AND SO I HURRIED ON.

HERE, MUMMY, THESE ARE FOR YOU...

THE PLASTIC BAG THAT HELD THE BREAD, THE ELECTRIC KETTLE...

THE ENTIRE KITCHEN WAS ALIEN TO THE WORLD THAT I HAD JUST LEFT.

DO YOU WANT SOME ORANGE SQUASH?

GO AND WASH YOUR HANDS AND FACE

IT'LL BE TIME FOR TEA AND THEN WE MUST GET GOING IN TIME FOR THE BUS.

IN THE SHINY PINK BATHROOM I CLEANED OFF MY WOUNDS AND PUT ON STRETCH PANTS TO COVER MY WELTS.

ALL WITHOUT LOOKING AROUND TO SEE ME

NOW GET RID OF ALL OF THE WILDFLOWERS.

BECAUSE THEY WILL DIE. THEY NEVER LAST.

I SADLY COLLECTED THE FLOWERS I HAD GATHERED AS A GIFT, CAREFUL NOT TO DRIP ON THE RUG.

CAN'T WE TAKE THEM HOME?

DON'T BE SILLY.

ANYWAY, WE HAVE ENOUGH TO CARRY.

AND TOMORROW YOU HAVE SCHOOL.

I'LL JUST MAKE A BUTTONHOLE THEN, AND TAKE OUT THE REST.

BUT SETTING THE TABLE FOR TEA HAD TAKEN OVER. THE OTHER WORLD FADED INTO DARKNESS.

Nature Lessons

ON RAINY DAYS, AND IT SEEMED THERE WERE ALL TOO MANY, WE BEGGED FOR THE WEATHER TO WORSEN.

IF THE WINDS GATHERED STRENGTH, WE FLEW DOWN TO THE SEA AND THREW OURSELVES, TINY MITES THAT WE WERE, INTO THE SEA TO BE CAST ABOUT ON THE WAVES.

THE SEA IS WARMER THAN THE AIR ON THOSE DAYS, AND THE SWELLING WAVES GIVE ONE THE ABILITY TO FLY.

ALONE IN THE VASTNESS OF THE SEA, THE BEACHES ABANDONED, WE OWNED THE WORLD.

IF STORM CLOUDS CROWDED THE SKY, SO MUCH THE BETTER.

AND WHEN THE THUNDER JOINED THE CRASHING WAVES TO PAINT THE WORLD A STRANGE ELECTRIC GREY

WE BAITED THE LIGHTNING TO ADD TO OUR THRILLS.

OVER AND OVER AGAIN, WE SWAM OUT TO BE DISEMBODIED BY THE SWELLS, AS THEY OVERTOOK OUR BODIES AND LET US RIDE INTO THE SHORE.

AND ALL THE WHILE, WE LAUGHED AND WHOOPED WITH DELIGHT, TWO LITTLE BERRY-BROWN BODIES IN PERFECT FRIENDSHIP.

THE ADULT WORLD WENT ABOUT ITS BUSINESS

IT NEVER NOTICED THAT WE WERE RISKING OUR LIVES IN THIS EXISTENTIAL GAME OF TAG WITH THE SEA.

YOU GIRLS MUST
BE FROZEN!

DRY OFF AND
YOU CAN HAVE
SOME HOT
MILK.

WE WOULD TAKE THE STAIRS
THREE AT A TIME UP TO THE
ENORMOUS BATHROOM.

AND CAST OFF OUR SHORTS AND
STILL-WET SWIMSUITS, PLUCKING
TINY STRANDS OF SEAWEED
FROM OUR CREVICES...

BEFORE PULLING ON OUR DRY THINGS
TO ZOOM DOWN TO THE KITCHEN.

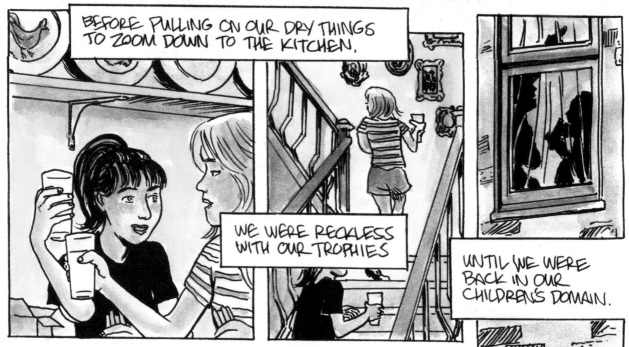

WE WERE RECKLESS
WITH OUR TROPHIES

UNTIL WE WERE
BACK IN OUR
CHILDREN'S DOMAIN.

WE DEVOTED OURSELVES TO
THE EATING AND ORDERING
OF BISCUITS FOR AS LONG AS
POSSIBLE, DEVISING NEW
WAYS TO MAKE THE PLEASURE
OF EACH CRUMB LAST LONGER.

WE DESPISED PINK DOLLS AND DRESSES. WE LIKED HAMSTERS. WE PUT THEM IN OUR SWEATERS AS WE RAN AND EXPLORED.

AT EIGHT YEARS OLD, IT IS POSSIBLE TO OUTRUN ALL THE BOYS IN ONE'S CLASS, TO OUTCLIMB THEM AND IN MOST CASES TO OUTDARE THEM.

PRUNELLA WAS MY HERO. I WAS NICKNAMED MAGGOT.

TOGETHER WE WERE A DELIGHT UNTO OURSELVES.

SHE WAS A CRACK BATTER AND BOWLER TOO. HER TWO OLDER BROTHERS LET US PLAY CRICKET WITH THEM.

WE WERE MOST OFTEN IN OUTFIELD, BUT THE BOYS GENUINELY LIKED US AND THERE WAS NO RIBBING FROM THAT QUARTER.

THE SUNNY DAYS ON THE LAWNS WIPED AWAY ANY CARES, LEAVING THE WARMTH OF COMPANIONSHIP TO MATCH THE HEAT ON OUR SKIN.

THOSE RARE DAYS WERE LIKE HONEY TO US.

NOT THAT WE HAD ANY CARES WHEN WE WERE TOGETHER. WE SLIPPED THEM OFF WITH OUR PARENTS' GAZE AND OUR SHOES AND SOCKS.

I THINK WE KNEW WELL ENOUGH THAT IT WAS SPECIAL, BUT WE NEVER SPOKE OF IT, BECAUSE WE UNDERSTOOD THE VULNERABILITY OF THE MOMENT. WE WOULD GROW UP AND CHANGE. EVENTUALLY WE WOULD LOSE EACH OTHER, NO MATTER HOW MANY PACTS OF FOREVER WE MADE.

FOR NOW, WE LIVED IN HAPPY STORIES OF OUR OWN DEVISING THAT MIRRORED THE BEST ADVENTURE STORIES WE READ AT BEDTIME.

THE DRIZZLE DIDN'T BOTHER HIM A BIT.

HE TOOK HIS PLACE IN THE SHADOWS ACROSS THE STREET FROM THE BUS DRIVERS AND MUNICIPAL TRANSPORT WORKERS' TRANSIT HALL.

HE COULDN'T BELIEVE HIS LUCK ON THE DAY HE DISCOVERED THAT IT HAD RENTED ITS ASSEMBLY ROOMS TO A SMALL DANCING SCHOOL.

RAIN TRICKLED SLOWLY DOWN HIS NECK AND SLIPPED BENEATH THE FRAY OF HIS SHIRT COLLAR.

HIS NECK WAS ALWAYS SLIGHTLY HOT BECAUSE THE BARBER'S RAZOR BURNT HIS SKIN. HE KEPT UP HIS SHORT BACK AND SIDES.

HE APPLIED BRYLCREEM TO MANAGE THE UNRULY BITS.

HE THOUGHT IT MADE A GOOD IMPRESSION.

HE WAS NOT LIKELY TO BE CHALLENGED AS A LAYABOUT LOOKING AS KEMPT AS HE DID.

HE DIDN'T LIKE TO BE NOTICED.

HE DIDN'T CONSIDER HIMSELF TO BE A LOUD MAN. IT WAS HELPFUL TO KEEP TO HIMSELF. HE DIDN'T ENJOY THE COMPANY OF OTHER MEN WHO TALKED RUBBISH AFTER A FEW BEERS. NOR DID FOOTBALL OR THE HORSES HOLD ANY CHARM.

HE WAS DIFFERENT.

AT FIRST HE THOUGHT IT WAS A PARTY THROWN FOR THE CHILDREN OF THE EMPLOYEES. ON HIS WAY TO THE FISH SHOP HE SAW FOUR LITTLE GIRLS IN THEIR PINK TIGHTS AND LEOTARDS AS THEY PLAYED A SORT OF DANCED GAME OF TAG.

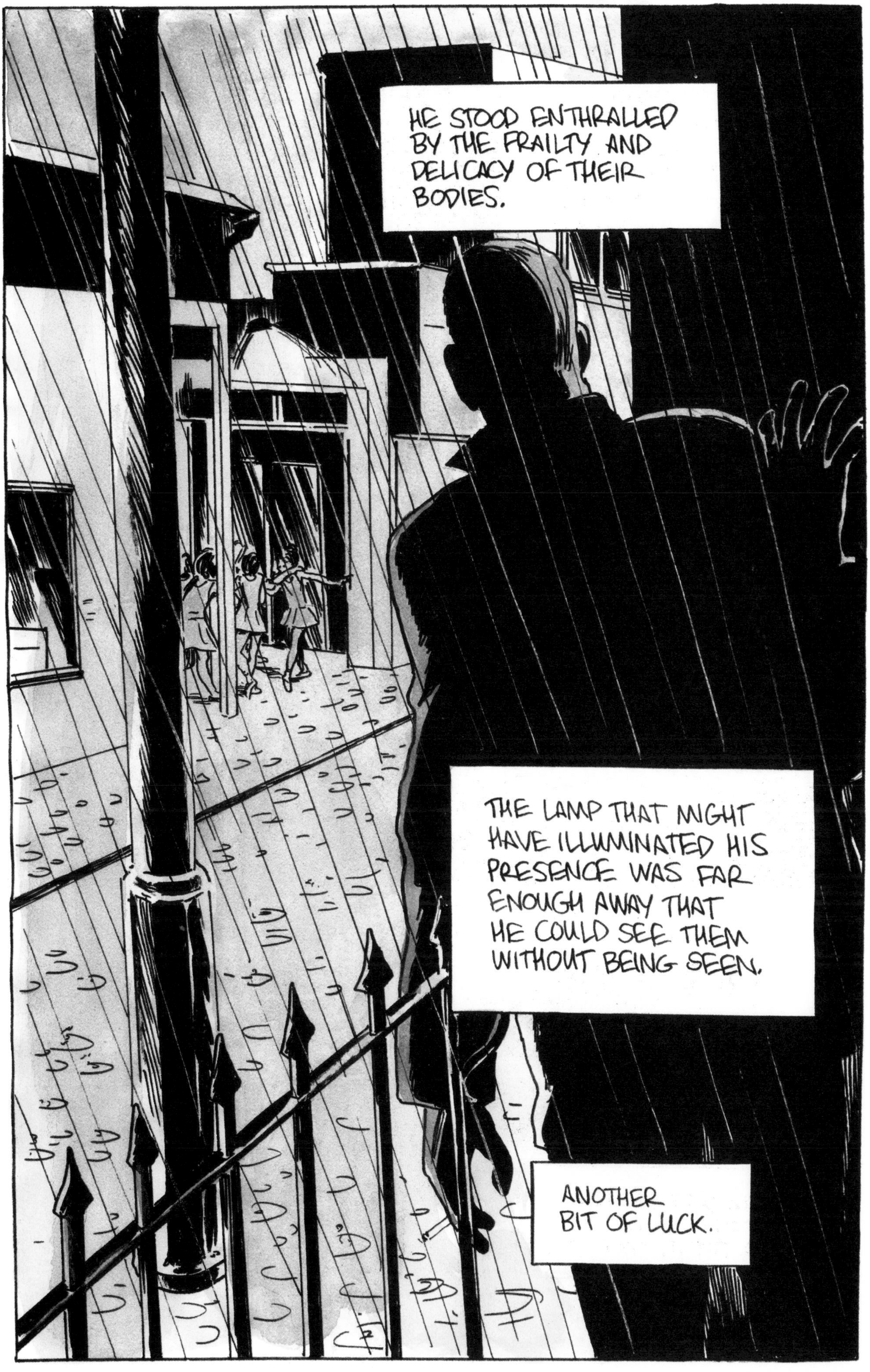
HE STOOD ENTHRALLED BY THE FRAILTY AND DELICACY OF THEIR BODIES.
THE LAMP THAT MIGHT HAVE ILLUMINATED HIS PRESENCE WAS FAR ENOUGH AWAY THAT HE COULD SEE THEM WITHOUT BEING SEEN.
ANOTHER BIT OF LUCK.

WHEN THE SUMMER INEVITABLY GIVES WAY TO THE FALL AND SCHOOL BELLS CALL CHILDREN ALONG LEAFY STREWN PAVEMENTS TO CLASS, GOODBYES ARE QUICKLY REPLACED BY A NEW CIRCLE OF HELLOS, AND RESILIENT CHILDREN SECRETLY EMBRACE THE COMING SCHOOL DAYS.

THUS IT IS WITH THOSE WHO HAVE MORE LIFE BEFORE THEM THAN BEHIND

SOUTHAMPTON CITY TRANSPORTS
LAST REAR PLATFORM BUS

ESPECIALLY THOSE WHO THINK THAT AN AGE WITH DOUBLE DIGITS SIGNIFIES GREAT AGE.

ALL THE CHILDREN ARE NAVY OFFICERS' CHILDREN.

OR PRO-FESSIONALS.

PRUNELLA LEFT FOR HER SCHOOL AND I WENT, AS MOTHER PUT IT, "OFF TO A SCHOOL THAT WAS BETTER THAN A PRIVATE SCHOOL."

WE WERE CODDLED IN OUR SMALL CLASSES LIKE THE ROBINS' EGGS IN COTTON WOOL THAT FILLED THE NATURE CORNER.

THE TINY SCHOOL HELD ONLY EIGHTY CHILDREN, IF THAT.

EVERY DAY, MR. EDWARDS READ TO US A NATURE STORY BY TED HUGHES FROM THE TIMES OR THE TELEGRAPH, VAST BROADSHEETS 'FROM OUR PERSPECTIVE.

I WAS IN AWE THAT THE ADULT WORLD CONCERNED ITSELF WITH FOXES' DENS AND VOLES IN THE HEDGEROWS.

"A FOX'S NOSE TOUCHES TWIG, LEAF..."

HUGHES HIMSELF SPOKE ON THE SCHOOL RADIO ONCE A WEEK.

"SETS NEAT PRINTS INTO THE SNOW BETWEEN THE TREES"

"AND WARILY, A LAME SHADOW LAGS BY STUMP AND IN HOLLOW.''

HE SOUNDED EMINENTLY REASONABLE, HIS KINDLY TALES BELYING THE DRAMA THAT PLAYED OUT IN HIS EMOTIONALLY CHARGED PERSONAL LIFE WITH SYLVIA PLATH. ON THE RADIO, AT LEAST, EVERYTHING WENT WELL.

ON TUESDAYS AND THURSDAYS AFTER SCHOOL AND ON SATURDAY MORNINGS I WENT TO MY DANCING CLASSES.

THE BUS RIDE WAS AT LEAST FORTY MINUTES TO THE OTHER SIDE OF TOWN.

WHEN THE BUSES WERE SLOW, I SOMETIMES CHANGED AT THE GUILD HALL, STOPPING AT THE LARGE EXPANSE BEFORE THE CITY HALL BUILDINGS, FLANKED BY THE PORTSMOUTH AND SOUTHSEA TRAIN STATION. BUT IT COST ME MORE, A WHOLE PENNY.

I PREFERRED TO BUY SWEETIES WITH WHATEVER CHANGE THAT I COULD GLEAN BY ECONOMY.

ALTHOUGH I FAR ADMIRED NUREYEV TO ANY FEMALE DANCERS FOR HIS GREAT LEAPS AND BOUNDS, I TRIED MY BEST TO ROUND MY WRISTS AND SOFTEN MY ARMS FOR BALLET.

I LIKED THE MODERN CLASSES BEST BECAUSE THEY THREW OFF THE CONSTRAINTS OF CLASSICAL DANCE.

I LOVED TO THROW MYSELF AROUND THE ROOM

AND FEEL THE RUSH OF THE AIR AS I FLEW AND SPUN

I CLACKED ABOUT IN TAP SHOES, TOO.

BUT MUM AND IRIS, MY DANCE TEACHER, DECIDED THAT I WOULD ENTER THE COMPETITIVE FESTIVALS,

IT REQUIRED THAT I LEARNED SOLO DANCES AND A DUET,

WHY THEY FAILED TO SEE THAT I WAS A TOM-BOY MYSTIFIED ME.

I LONGED FOR A MODERN DANCE, BUT BECAUSE I WAS SO SLIGHT AND ETHEREAL IT WAS DECIDED THAT I SHOULD HAVE A SLOWER NUMBER INVOLVING A LOT OF LONG, HARD-TO-HOLD POSES.

ALL I WANTED THEM TO SEE WAS THAT I WAS A BOLT OF EXPLOSIVE ENERGY.

I PRACTICED THAT SKILL DILIGENTLY.

SADLY, THEY MADE ME SING SOPPY SONGS TOO, BECAUSE I WAS ABLE TO MAKE PEOPLE CRY.

THE MOTHERS ALL CAME WITH THEIR HANKIES OUT, READY TO HEAR ME. BUT OUTSIDE AT PLAY, I SCREAMED, YELLED, AND RAN AS FEROCIOUSLY AS ANY OF MY DANCE SCHOOL FRIENDS.

WHEN CLASS WAS OVER, IT WAS USUALLY A LONG DARK RIDE HOME ON THE BUS.

I DIDN'T LIKE THE WALK TO THE BUS STOP. IT WAS DARK AND EMPTY.

LIFE HAPPENED IN THE OTHER DIRECTION.

THE SHOPS WERE ALL CLOSED AT SIX AND MOST OF THE BUILDINGS ON THE STREET HAD NEVER BEEN UNBOARDED SINCE THE WAR.

I WAS ALWAYS GLAD TO MEET THE MAIN ROAD, ALTHOUGH THE STOP WAS IN FRONT OF AN OLD ABANDONED HOUSE.

THE EVERGREEN THAT PUSHED THROUGH THE FENCE SEEMED TO SWALLOW LIGHT.

I IMAGINED GHOSTS READY TO POP OUT. THE SIGHT OF PASSING CARS REASSURED ME.

THE FIRST TIME, HE INDULGED HIMSELF WITH A BAG OF CHIPS FROM THE FISH SHOP AND STOOD EATING THEM PIPING HOT FROM THE NEWSPAPER.

THE SMELL OF VINEGAR WAS A PLEASURE, BUT THE GREASE ON HIS FINGERS MADE HIM UNCOMFORTABLE.

AND HE DIDN'T WANT TO BECOME KNOWN AT THE SHOP, SO HE NEVER ALLOWED HIMSELF THAT TREAT AGAIN.

SOMETIMES, DURING THE FIRST FEW DAYS OF DISCOVERY, HIS STOMACH BECAME SO KNOTTED WITH PLEASURE THAT HE COULDN'T HAVE EATEN IF HE WANTED TO.

THE CHURNING TURMOIL IN HIS GUT HEIGHTENED HIS SELF-AWARENESS.

SACRIFICES MUST BE MADE IN SERVICE OF HIS TASK AND HE STOPPED EATING AT ALL SOME DAYS.

IT MADE HIM A LITTLE LIGHT-HEADED, BUT HE QUITE LIKED THE SENSATION.

AS THE MONTH PASSED, HE THOUGHT HE'D BETTER KEEP HIS WITS ABOUT HIM, SO HE BROUGHT A SANDWICH METICULOUSLY WRAPPED IN TINFOIL.

KEPT IN HIS POCKET UNTIL 5:30, BEAMED IN NEON FROM A TINY HIGH WINDOW OF THE TRANSPORT CLUB.

THE GIRLS WERE ALL IN CLASS FOR ANOTHER HALF HOUR BEFORE THEY CAME OUT. THE CLOCK GAVE HIM A WAY TO EKE OUT THE MOMENTS AS HE FANTASIZED ABOUT HIS UPCOMING REWARD.

AND IT MADE HIM LAUGH THAT THE ONLY VISIBLE PART OF THE CLUB WAS A TIMEPIECE.

THE BUSES NEVER RAN ON TIME.

BUT THAT WAS A GOOD THING IN PART.

SOMETHING UPON WHICH HE WAS DEPENDING.

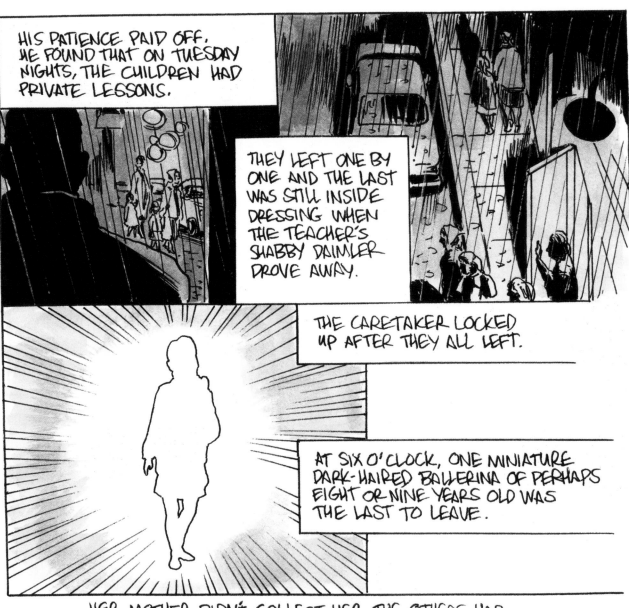

HIS PATIENCE PAID OFF. HE FOUND THAT ON TUESDAY NIGHTS, THE CHILDREN HAD PRIVATE LESSONS.

THEY LEFT ONE BY ONE AND THE LAST WAS STILL INSIDE DRESSING WHEN THE TEACHER'S SHABBY DAIMLER DROVE AWAY.

THE CARETAKER LOCKED UP AFTER THEY ALL LEFT.

AT SIX O'CLOCK, ONE MINIATURE DARK-HAIRED BALLERINA OF PERHAPS EIGHT OR NINE YEARS OLD WAS THE LAST TO LEAVE.

HER MOTHER DIDN'T COLLECT HER. THE OTHERS HAD DRAB HAGS TO PICK THEM UP AND DRAG THEM OFF.

HE WATCHED THE LIPSTICK-SMEARED COWS SQUAWKING ABUSE AT HIS GIRLS

THEY PASSED BEYOND, INTO THE NARROW ROW OF HOUSES AND THE CROWDING SLUMS TO THE CITY CENTER

BUT HIS GIRL WENT THE OTHER WAY

SHE WENT TO THE EMPTY MAIN ROAD WHERE THE SHOPS CLOSE AT SIX TO WAIT FOR THE 145, THE ANTIQUE RED BUS THAT ONLY CAME BUT ONCE EVERY FIFTEEN MINUTES

IF SHE MISSED IT

OR IF IT RAN LATE, AS IT OFTEN DID

UP TO HALF AN HOUR LATE

THEN HE COULD HAVE ALL OF THE TIME IN THE WORLD

WITH HER

ALL HE HAD TO DO WAS SLOW HER DOWN

AND HE WOULD HAVE PLENTY OF TIME

BUT ON THE ORIGINAL TUESDAY HE PLANNED TO MEET HIS GIRL, HE WAS FORCED TO RUN AN ERRAND FOR HIS MOTHER. SHE MADE HIM GO TO THE CHEMIST FOR SOMETHING TO EASE HER SWELLED LEGS, OR SHE'D NEVER GIVE HIM ANY PEACE.

BUT IT WAS THEN THAT HE HAD HIS GOOD IDEA.

HE RETURNED HOME SMILING.

"NUFFINK, MUM. I'M JUST PLEASED TO MAKE YOU 'APPY."

AND HE LEANED FORWARD TO KISS HER, SOMETHING HE HADN'T DONE FOR A LONG TIME.

"YORE FULL 'A BEANS," SAID HIS MOTHER. "WOT'S MADE YOU SO HAPPY?"

AFTERWARDS, IT MADE HIM SICK.

SHE'S JUST THE GIRL FOR ME

BUT HE WAS SO BUOYED UP IN HIS ANTICIPATION THAT WHEN HE SPIT OUT THE SALT WATER HE GARGLED WITH TO REMOVE ALL TRACES OF HIS MUM'S SMELLS, HE BEGAN TO HUM.

AN IDEA HAD COME INTO HIS MIND AND HE TURNED ON THE RADIO. THE BEATLES WERE SINGING THEIR HIT.

HAD IT BEEN ANOTHER DAY

I MIGHT HAVE LOOKED THE OTHER WAY

IF HE KNEW SOME POP SONGS, HE COULD STRIKE UP A MORE NATURAL CONVERSATION. WHAT COULD BE BETTER?

NA, NA NA NA NA NA

THAT NIGHT, HIS MIND HAD BEEN FILLED WITH THOUGHTS ABOUT THIS GIRL AND WHAT HE WOULD SAY.

HE MARVELLED AT HOW PETITE AND GRACEFUL SHE WAS,

JUST A LITTLE DOLL. BIG GREEN EYES AND FULL PINK MOUTH.

HE WIGGLED HIS COLD TOES WITH SHIVERS OF GLEE.

ONCE, HE HAD HEARD HER CALLING TO THE OTHERS. SHE SPOKE DIFFERENTLY THAN THE OTHER GIRLS.

SHE WAS POSHER.

IT ADDED SOMETHING.

HE'D TAKE HER DOWN AND SHOW HER WHO WAS ON TOP.

LUVLY.

106

FROM HIS PERCH, THE BLACK BIRD WATCHED AS THE LITTLE GIRL WALKED TOWARDS THE WAY OUT. HE SAW THE MAN ACROSS THE STREET, AND HE BROKE THE SILENCE, NOT TO WARN THE GIRL, BECAUSE HE WAS A BIRD AND BIRDS RARELY MEDDLE IN THE BUSINESS OF MEN.

K'KAAAW! KAAAW!

HEY!

HOLD UP, THERE!

THE LITTLE GIRL, WHO KNEW SHE MUST NOT SPEAK TO STRANGERS, WAS NONETHELESS FORCED TO STOP, BECAUSE SHE WAS RAISED TO BE POLITE TO ADULTS.

ANY ADULT MUST HAVE A GOOD REASON TO STOP HER.

HELLO

I'M WALKING YOUR WAY

PERHAPS WE CAN WALK TOGETHER?

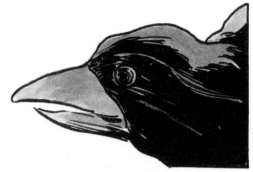

THE BIRD SAW THE CHILD HESITATE

THEN IT FLEW DOWN TO GRAB THE SANDWICH CRUMBS FROM WHERE THE MAN HAD STOOD

NOW IT WAS ALL HAPPENING. JUST AS HE HAD IMAGINED THAT IT WOULD

THE LITTLE GIRL WAS EVEN LOVELIER UP CLOSE

SMALLER, PINKER

HE COULD ALMOST SMELL HER

COME ON NOW. NOT YET

YOU ARE LETTING YOURSELF RUN AWAY WITH THINGS

HE FELT BLOOD RUSHING TO HIS FACE AND EXPOSED EARS AS HE APPROACHED HER

WHAT'S YOUR NAME?

I MUST GO NOW.

I'M GOING TO MISS MY BUS.

OH, I KNOW THAT.

I'LL WALK WITH YOU

I KNOW YOUR DAD.

HE WAS SO CLOSE NOW, HE COULD BARELY CONTAIN HIMSELF.

I WAS JUST WONDERING, SINCE YOU ARE GOING TO GET THE BUS...

WHETHER YOU WOULDN'T MIND CARRYING A PACKAGE FOR ME?

I WAS GOING TO GET THE BUS TOO.

BUT SINCE YOU ARE GOING...

HIS PRINCESS LOOKED WORRIED

NO, I'M SORRY...

HER SWEET VOICE THRILLED HIM

HE FELT HIS PRICK COME LOOSE OF THE FOLD IN HIS TROUSERS THAT HAD HELD IT DOWN

IT BEGAN TO SEARCH FOR TWELVE O'CLOCK, FOR THE RIGHT TIME

THE CHILD BEGAN TO WALK, BUT HE WAS CLOSE ENOUGH TO WALK BESIDE HER

THE STREET WAS COMPLETELY EMPTY

HE WATCHED HER AS THOUGH SHE WERE A SPINNING TOP

HIS HEAD WOVE CREEPILY, AS HE TRIED TO GAIN A DIRECT PATH TO HER EYES

SHE KEPT THEM AVERTED

HE ENJOYED HER CONFUSION.

BUT HE WASN'T DRESSED RIGHT

HE WASN'T SOMEHOW PROPER

SHE WAS BLINDSIDED AS TO HOW HE COULD KNOW ABOUT HER LIFE. PERHAPS HE **DID** KNOW HER FATHER.

THE SLIGHTEST TRACES OF FEAR BETRAYED THE CHILD'S DETERMINATION.

HE OPENED HIS LUNGS TO BREATHE HER IN.

BUT GROWNUPS, AND ESPECIALLY HER DAD, KNEW ALL KINDS OF PEOPLE.

THIS IS BETTER

MORE LIKE IT

DO YOU HAVE ANY SISTERS?

YES

WAVES OF EXCITEMENT SWARMED HIS BODY.

DO THEY HAVE NICE HAIR LIKE YOU?

OH, MY SISTER HAS VERY LONG HAIR, SHE CAN SIT ON IT.

NO, I MEAN BETWEEN THE LEGS.

YOU KNOW, DOWN THERE

THE BUS KIOSK WAS EMPTY. NO CARS TURNED DOWN FROM THE CROSSROADS

DO YOU LIKE BOYS?

HAVE YOU

I KNEW I WAS IN TROUBLE

ONE?

NO ONE CAME

HAVE YOU EVER SEEN A MAN'S THING?

HIS COCK, YEAH?

NO ONE STOPPED

HAVE YOU EVER KISSED ONE?

JUST A LITTLE FURTHER

I SILENTLY BEGGED FOR A STRANGER TO WHOM I COULD APPEAL

I COULDN'T BELIEVE THE NASTY THINGS HE WAS SAYING TO ME

COME ON, WE HAVE TO HURRY

YOUR DAD WILL WORRY

I WALKED ALONG, ONLY UNDERSTANDING THAT I WAS GOING TO BE TREATED VERY BADLY

I KNEW ABOUT SPIES AND TORTURE FROM WAR STORIES. WE USED TO PLAY JERRIES AND BRITS ON THE BOMBSITES, AND I PRACTICED ESCAPING OFTEN ENOUGH.

I WOKE FROM NIGHTMARES OF TORTURE AND HERE IT WAS, JUST LIKE THAT.

A NAZI TAKING A BRIT OFF TO DO UNSPEAKABLE THINGS.

IF I TRIED TO GET AWAY NOW, HE'D DEFINITELY CATCH ME.

AT LAST I PRETENDED TO GO WITH HIM. I THOUGHT IT MIGHT LOWER HIS GUARD.

WANNA HOLD HANDS?

NO, THANK YOU.

HA HA HA

MY VOICE CAME OUT TOO LOUD AND I TRIED TO SWALLOW THE SOUND. HE JINGLED THE CHANGE IN HIS POCKET.

CHING

CHINK

THIS IS FOR YOU IF YOU DO ME THIS FAVOR

HELP

I NEED SOMEBODY

HE BEGAN SINGING A BEATLES SONG

DO YOU LIKE THAT?

WHY DON'T YOU SING IT?

WON'T YOU PLEASE

HE THOUGHT IT WAS FUNNY

PLEASE HELP ME

HELP ME HELP ME-E-YEAH

WE'RE ALMOST THERE. NOT VERY FAR OFF THE WAY.

YOU DON'T WANT TO LET YOUR DAD DOWN NOW, DO YOU?

DO YOU HAVE BATHS WITH YOUR DAD?

DOES HE WASH YOU ALL AROUND THE HOUSES?

HE SAID THINGS I DIDN'T KNOW. THE WORDS WERE SICKENING.

NO ONE IN MY LIFE HAD EVER SAID WORDS LIKE THESE. HE TOWERED OVER ME.

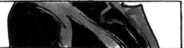

THINGS BECAME VERY DIRE.

IF HE KNEW FOR SURE THAT I UNDERSTOOD WHAT HE HAD IN MIND, THE GAME WOULD END.

I HAD TO PRETEND.

I HAD TO ESCAPE.

WE APPROACHED THE END OF THE MAIN ROAD.

SMALL ERUPTIONS POPPED IN THE GAS WORKS.

BOOM

IF HE GOT ME TO THE DOCKS, I WAS DEAD.

I KNEW IT.

BUT DEATH WASN'T THE WORST THING THAT LOOMED BEFORE ME.

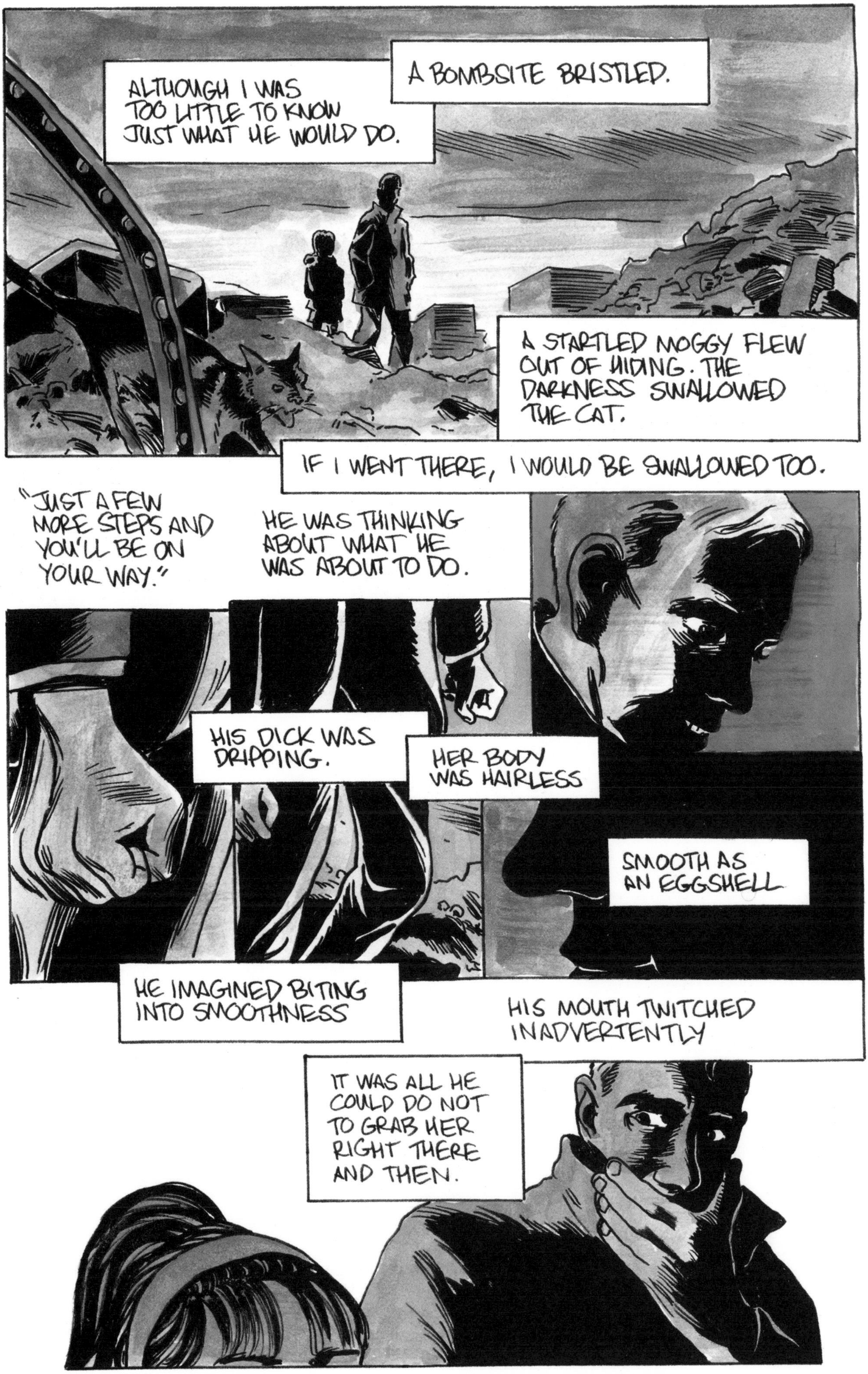

ALTHOUGH I WAS TOO LITTLE TO KNOW JUST WHAT HE WOULD DO.
A BOMBSITE BRISTLED.
A STARTLED MOGGY FLEW OUT OF HIDING. THE DARKNESS SWALLOWED THE CAT.
IF I WENT THERE, I WOULD BE SWALLOWED TOO.
"JUST A FEW MORE STEPS AND YOU'LL BE ON YOUR WAY."
HE WAS THINKING ABOUT WHAT HE WAS ABOUT TO DO.
HIS DICK WAS DRIPPING.
HER BODY WAS HAIRLESS
SMOOTH AS AN EGGSHELL
HE IMAGINED BITING INTO SMOOTHNESS
HIS MOUTH TWITCHED INADVERTENTLY
IT WAS ALL HE COULD DO NOT TO GRAB HER RIGHT THERE AND THEN.

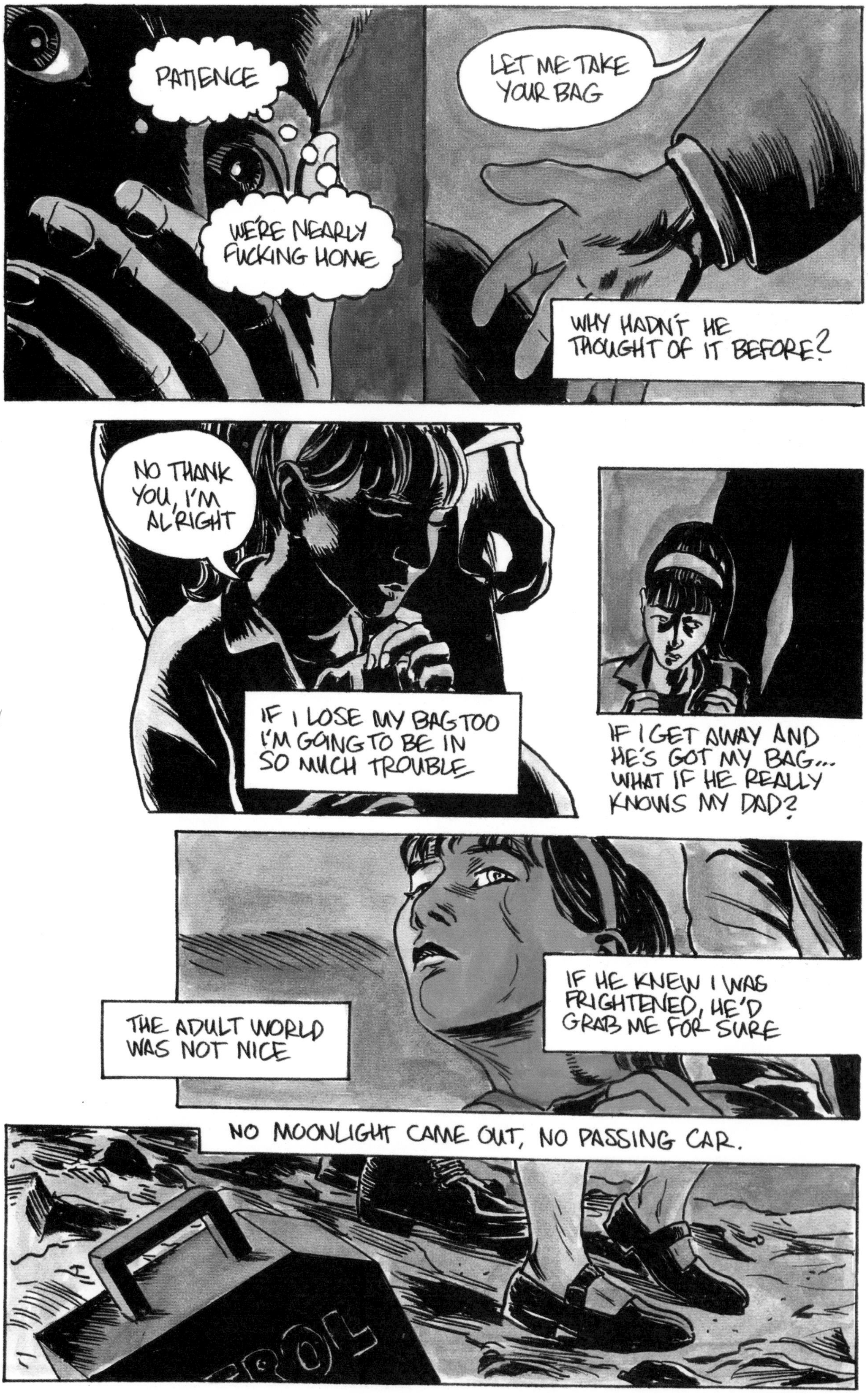
PATIENCE
WE'RE NEARLY FUCKING HOME
LET ME TAKE YOUR BAG
WHY HADN'T HE THOUGHT OF IT BEFORE?
NO THANK YOU, I'M AL'RIGHT
IF I LOSE MY BAG TOO I'M GOING TO BE IN SO MUCH TROUBLE
IF I GET AWAY AND HE'S GOT MY BAG... WHAT IF HE REALLY KNOWS MY DAD?
THE ADULT WORLD WAS NOT NICE
IF HE KNEW I WAS FRIGHTENED, HE'D GRAB ME FOR SURE
NO MOONLIGHT CAME OUT, NO PASSING CAR.

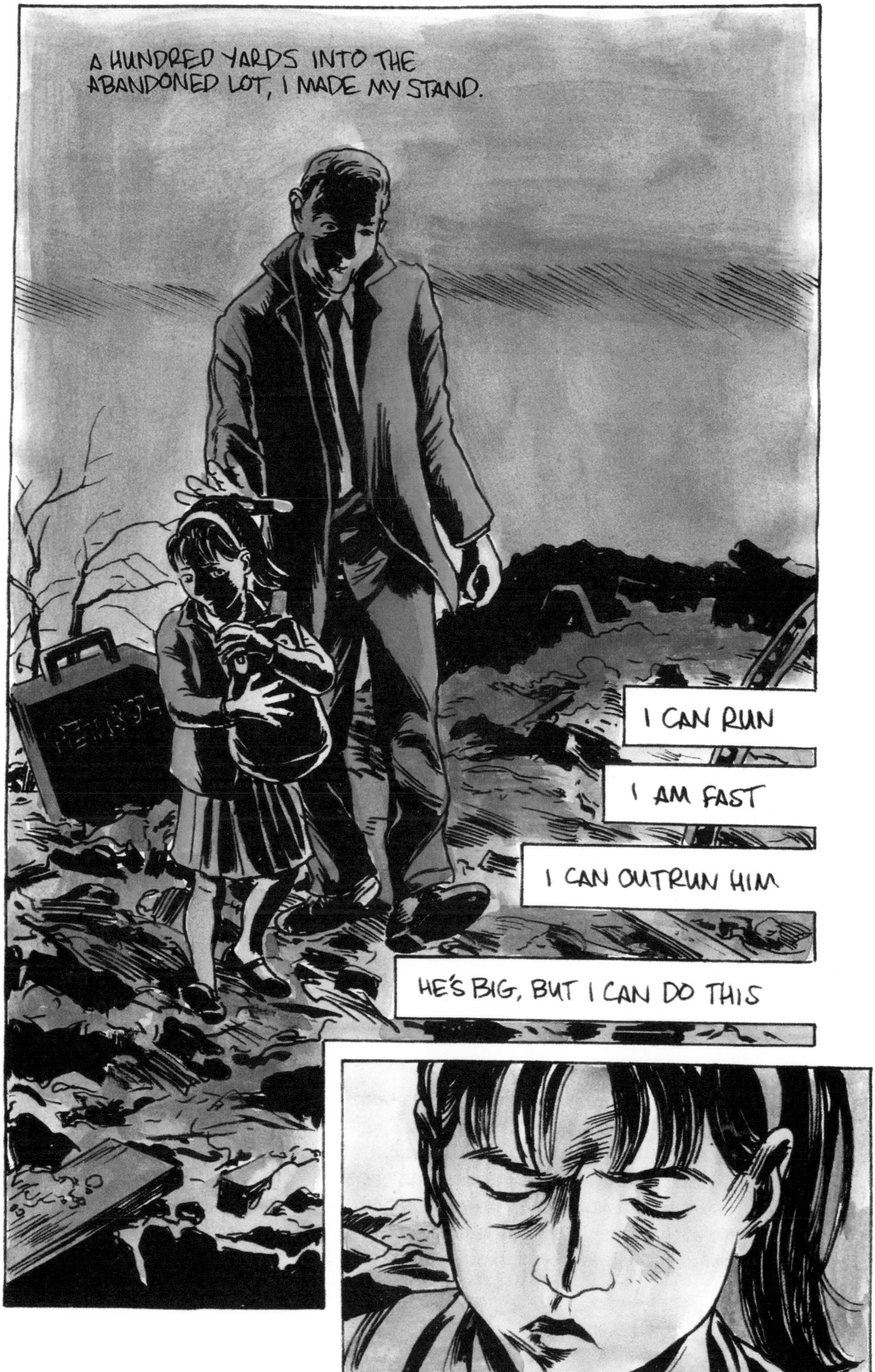
A HUNDRED YARDS INTO THE ABANDONED LOT, I MADE MY STAND.
I CAN RUN
I AM FAST
I CAN OUTRUN HIM
HE'S BIG, BUT I CAN DO THIS

I KICKED HIM AS HARD AS I COULD IN THE SHINS

HE DIDN'T EXPECT IT

HEY!

I RAN, BECAUSE I WAS FASTER THAN THE BOYS AND I COULD RUN.

I STARTED TOWARDS PEOPLE, TOWARDS LIFE.

TEARS CAME NOW

I DIDN'T LOOK TO SEE IF HE WAS FOLLOWING ME.

I COULDN'T SPARE THE BREATH TO CRY FOR HELP.

THEN I PUT THE OIL CAN BETWEEN US

I SAW HIM LUNGE AND STUMBLE

IT WAS ALL I NEEDED TO GET A HEAD START

MY DAD TOLD ME NEVER TO LOOK BACK IN A RACE, AND THIS WAS THE RACE FOR MY LIFE. I DIDN'T LOOK BACK, I RAN.

I RAN FOR MILES

I PRESSED ON LIKE A DEER

I RAN STRAIGHT WHEN I COULD FIND THE CROW'S PATH

FINALLY, I SAW THE LIGHT OF A PUB AND FOUND MY VOICE..

BUT THE DOORS DIDN'T OPEN

IF HE'S STILL BEHIND ME...

AND I KNOW HE IS... HE WILL KILL ME BECAUSE HE KNOWS THAT I'LL TELL.

DON'T LOOK BACK.

NOW THERE WERE A FEW ODD PEOPLE

I COULDN'T STOP

I WAS CALLING

BUT NO ONE ASKED ME, "WHAT'S WRONG, LITTLE GIRL?"

NO ONE STOPPED ME TO PROTECT ME

I WAS IN A FRENZY OF FEAR

MY SOUL'S DISAPPOINTMENT FLOWED OUT WITH MY TEARS.

I KEPT CALLING FOR HELP, BUT NO ONE BUDGED.

MY BUS WAS AT THE STOP AT THE GUILDHALL SQUARE

I LEAPT ON AND TOOK A SEAT NEXT TO THE CONDUCTOR.

NOW I MIGHT HAVE TO SAY THOSE WORDS

THEY HAD SOILED ME

IT WAS ONLY THEN THAT I LOOKED BACK

I COULDN'T SEE HIM

THEY STUCK TO ME

I COULDN'T SAY THOSE SHAMEFUL THINGS

I SAT, TOO EMBARRASSED TO ASK FOR HELP ANYMORE

I PERCHED ON THE SEAT WITH ACUTE FEAR

WHAT IF THE MAN PRETENDED THAT I WAS HIS CHILD?

WHAT IF HE GOT ON THE BUS?

BUT THE BUS PULLED OUT WITHOUT INCIDENT.

THE YELLOW LIGHTS ON THE RED BAIZE SEATS FILLED ME WITH FAMILIAR RELIEF.

ON THE HIGH STREET, THE CONDUCTOR CALLED, "NEXT STOP, CATHEDRAL."

THE BUS PULLED UP AND I RAN THE HALF BLOCK TO MY HOUSE.

MUM HAD JUST COME IN HERSELF.

MUMMY, A MAN TRIED TO TAKE ME AWAY!

"COME HERE, LOVE," SAID MUM AND SHE HELD ME.

SHE WET A WASH CLOTH AND WIPED MY FACE WITH BLESSED WARM WATER.

I TOLD HER PART OF MY ORDEAL. I COULDN'T BRING MYSELF TO SAY IT ALL. SHE LISTENED SILENTLY. SHE WAS UPSET...

BUT SHE DIDN'T BETRAY WHAT PARTICULAR EMOTION SHE FELT.

I'LL CALL RAY GILLON.

HE'S AN EX-POLICEMAN.

HE'LL KNOW WHAT TO DO.

YOU CAN SLEEP IN MY BED TONIGHT.

I'VE PUT THE ELECTRIC BLANKET ON FOR YOU.

I CLIMBED INTO HER BED, SHAKY FROM THE ORDEAL

ON HER BEDSIDE TABLE WAS "THE WATER BABIES."

I FELT KINDRED TO THE LITTLE CHIMNEY SWEEPS IN THE TALE WHO FALL TO THE BOTTOM OF THE POND TO BE FINALLY FREE OF THE SOOT OF THE MODERN WORLD

THE WORLD WHERE ADULTS HAVE ABUSED THEM.

MOTHER MADE ME MILKY COFFEE AND I SAT UP IN BED AND WAITED FOR NEWS.

NONE EVER CAME.

IT IS ONLY IN LATER YEARS THAT I REALIZED HOW MANY REASONS THERE WERE FOR A SINGLE MOTHER NOT TO MAKE A FUSS ABOUT THAT NASTY BUSINESS.

SOMETIMES I TASTED THE BILE OF HIS WORDS IN MY MOUTH AND BECAUSE I WAS TOO POLITE TO SPIT, I'D HAVE TO SWALLOW HIS POISON.

ALL THOSE FACES JUST BLURRED BY ME. NOT ONE REACHED OUT TO SHARE MY PROBLEMS.

IN TRUTH, THE AUTHORITIES WOULD HAVE GIVEN MOTHER HELL, BECAUSE SHE LET ME GO TO DANCE CLASSES ALONE, AND MAYBE THEY WOULD'VE TAKEN ME AWAY.

A SINGLE UNMARRIED MOTHER WAS FAIR GAME.

IT WOULD HAVE MADE THE LOCAL PAPER, AT THE VERY LEAST.

SHE NEVER BROUGHT IT UP AGAIN. PERHAPS SHE FELT GUILTY.

BUT THEN AGAIN, IT WAS SO MUCH MORE CONVENIENT WHEN SHE WAS FREE OF ME, EVEN FOR A FEW HOURS...

NOT TO HAVE HER OWN SHAME TO BEAR.

PERHAPS ALL THOSE CLASSES MADE ME A GOOD DANCER.

PERHAPS, I FANTASIZED AS I PIROUETTED ON THE CATHEDRAL LAWN

SOMEONE WILL NOTICE ME

AND THINK, WHAT A BEAUTIFUL CHILD

AND TAKE ME OFF TO DANCE ON THE STAGE

THAT NASTY MAN MAY OR MAY NOT HAVE BEEN CAUGHT

STRANGELY, I KEPT GOING ON MY OWN TO DANCE CLASS

FOR A WHILE, THEY MADE SURE THAT SOMEONE WALKED ME TO THE BUS STOP.

BUT SOON THEY FORGOT

AND IN NO TIME, I WAS WALKING THAT STREET WITH THE CROW IGNORING ME.

WHEN I WAS VERY AFRAID, I'D SING AT THE TOP OF MY LUNGS.

JUST TO MAKE SURE THAT NO ONE THOUGHT I WAS A NICE QUIET LITTLE GIRL EVER AGAIN.

Maupassant Compris

THE PARIS RIOTS OF MAY FUELED OUR IMAGINATIONS, BUT ONLY LIGHTLY.

THE FLYING COBBLESTONES AND THE WILD DEMOS BELONGED TO ANOTHER GENERATION.

WE WERE TOO YOUNG TO BE PART OF THAT WORLD OF PROTEST.

IT MEANT NOTHING TO US. WE WERE TOO CHILDISH TO BE POLITICIZED.

THE DRAMA THAT SEIZED THE ATTENTION OF THE WORLD, THOUGH PASSIONATE, DID NOT SPEAK DIRECTLY OF LOVE.

IF THEY HAD BEEN FIGHTING FOR THE RIGHT TO BE IN LOVE, IT WOULD HAVE MEANT MORE TO US.

ON THE STREETS, THE STUDENTS SHOOED US ALONG; THEY TOO TREATED US LIKE CHILDREN.

THEY FAILED TO SEE US AS FEELING PEOPLE.

FOR US, THEY JOINED THE GREAT *THEM* OF OTHERNESS.

WE WERE INTERESTED IN BOYS AND LIPSTICK, POETRY AND CIGARETTES, FASCINATED BY UGLY SERGE GAINSBOURG AND BEAUTIFUL JANE BIRKIN, IN ROMEO AND JULIET...

...AND OURSELVES.

THE SORT WE GRASPED FROM "BONJOUR TRISTESSE" BY THE YOUTHFUL FRANCOISE SAGAN.

PERHAPS A COPY OF "THE VIRGIN AND THE GYPSY."

WE DISCUSSED WHAT WOULD BE MOST VALUABLE ON A DESERT ISLAND: MASCARA OR A HAIRBRUSH. PERHAPS, AFTER ALL, A LIGHTER FOR FIRE AND FOR THE GESTURE OF LIGHTING THE STYLISH OBJECT...

WE WERE THE FIRST TO UNDERSTAND THE PROFUNDITY AND MEANING OF PURE LOVE.

I TENDED TO LEAN TOWARDS MASCARA, HAVING COMMITTED THE GIST OF D.H. LAWRENCE TO MEMORY.

YOU KNOW, THE WHOLE POINT IS THAT EVERYONE IS ALWAYS TELLING EVERYONE WHAT TO DO.

EVEN WHEN IT COMES TO LOVE...

WHY CAN'T WE ALL JUST LOVE THE PERSON THAT WE WANT TO?

AND THEN ALL OF THIS WOULD BECOME SO MUCH EASIER.

DO YOU THINK THAT THE SEXUAL ACT IS DISGUSTING?

I HATE MEN WITH HAIR ON THEIR CHESTS.

IT'S SO FOUL.

CAN YOU IMAGINE KISSING A MAN WITH A MOUSTACHE?

OR THEIR EARS

I WOULD HATE TO BE CALLED PRETTY

I THINK BEAUTIFUL HAS MORE DEPTH

SO MUCH MORE ETERNAL

WHAT SCARF ARE YOU TAKING?

I'M PACKING MY YELLOW FLOATY SCARF

TO GO WITH MY BLACK LACE BLOUSE.

BEAUTY WAS A PREMIUM.

IN CASE WE GO ANYWHERE.

CATHERINE'S ROOM WAS POWDER BLUE WITH LOUIS SEIZE FURNISHINGS. A GLASS BUILT-IN CABINET HELD A HOST OF PEYNET DOLLS. THEY WERE NOT TO BE TOUCHED.

THEY WERE EXQUISITE.

WE OCCUPIED THE ROOM, UNABLE TO TOUCH OUR OWN FURNITURE, LIKE A MIRROR OF THE LITTLE FIGURES.

AT ANY MOMENT, CATHERINE'S MOTHER WOULD COME TO SMOOTH THE SHANTUNG SILK DRAPERIES INTO MAGAZINE PERFECTION.

OUTSIDE ON THE STREET, REVOLUTION WENT ON.

INDOORS, WE BEGAN OUR OWN REVOLUTION...

LA CAUSE

AS WE LAUNCHED OUR SENSES OUT OF CHILDHOOD AND DEMANDED THE RIGHT TO TOUCH.

IN LATE JULY, WE LEFT PARIS FOR THE SEASON, SOON AFTER THE RIOTS WOUND DOWN.

THE FAMILY TOOK ME WITH THEM TO THEIR SEASIDE HOLIDAY HOME ON THE NORTHERN FRENCH COAST.

AS THE CITROËN DROVE DOWN THE MOTORWAYS, THE MALE SMELLS OF SCOTCH, GARLIC, AND GAULOISES MADE US SEEK THE REFUGE OF THE WIND.

INEVITABLY, THE WINDOW MUST BE CLOSED.

YVONNE'S HAIR MUST PRESERVE ITS RIGIDITY...

...A STYLE WE DISLIKED, AS IT LACKED NATURAL BEAUTY.

FROM OUR PLUSH BACK SEAT, WE SCOURED THE LANDSCAPE FOR SIGNS OF NATURAL BEAUTY.

WE SOUGHT IMAGES THAT REMINDED US OF PAINTINGS IN THE TUILERIES, PRINCIPALLY THE IMPRESSIONISTS.

THE ARTISTS' LIVES SEEMED SO ROMANTIC, BUT ALSO INSPIRED BY TRUTH AND THE BRUTALITY OF REALISM.

THE DRIVE PAUSED ONCE IN A WHILE.

UN SAND-WICH?

BUT MICHEL LIKED TO PULL ON THROUGH. HE DROVE WITH A CHEERFUL TENACITY.

ENSCONCED IN THE SYNTHETIC LUXURY OF THE SILVER CRAFT, ITS HYDRAULIC SUSPENSION GAVE IT AN UNEARTHLY SMOOTHNESS. WE GLIDED THROUGH THE NARROW ROADS.

BUT THE COWS WERE WHERE THEY SHOULD BE. NATURE WAS EN POINTE IN THE GREEN FIELDS.

FINALLY, WE ARRIVED IN THE NORMAN VILLAGE TO VILLA KINKON, A RED AND WHITE BUNGALOW.

THIS YEAR, IT SEEMED SMALLER.

CATHERINE AND I WERE IN PUBERTY, BUT HER PARENTS REFUSED TO SEE OUR TRANSFORMING BODIES.

THEY WANTED TO KEEP US CHILDREN ONE YEAR LONGER.

BUT WE ONLY WENT THROUGH THE MOTIONS OF PLAY AND WHISPERED SECRETIVELY.

AS WE PLANNED OUR ESCAPE FROM THEIR SURVEILLANCE.

THE LESSON WE TOOK FROM THE RIOTS WAS THAT THERE WAS THEM, AND THERE WAS US.

BUT, OUR METHOD OF OPPOSITION WAS FAR STEALTHIER THAN THAT OF THE STUDENTS.

WE WAITED FOR THE INEVITABLE MOMENTS WHEN THE ADULTS WOULD NOT BE LOOKING WITH SECRET SMILES OF ANTICIPATION.

BY THE CREPE STAND, A SMALL GANG OF TEENAGED BOYS HUNG OVER THEIR VELOS' HANDLEBARS.

SYMBOLS OF FREEDOM FROM THE ADULT WORLD.

AS IF BY MAGIC, YVONNE SENSED OUR EXCITEMENT.

ALORS, LES FILLÉS.

CE N'EST PAS LA PEINE D'Y ALLER.

THOSE BOYS ARE RUFFIANS.

AND I WILL BE VERY ANGRY IF I SEE YOU THERE.

I DON'T SUPPOSE YOU PLANNED TO GO THERE, BUT FOR TO MAKE ME HAPPY ...EH?

OH, C'MON YVONNE.

WE AREN'T EVEN OUT OF THE CAR.

LEAVE THE GIRLS ALONE.

IT'S A BIT MUCH.

I JUST WANT EVERYTHING TO BE AS IT SHOULD.

CATHERINE'S MOTHER, YVONNE, WAS A SMALL, TIDY WOMAN, UNLIKE CATHERINE, WHO WAS ALREADY VERY TALL AND LITHE.

YVONNE WAS A NORMAN.

CATHERINE'S FATHER, MICHEL, WAS A BIG MAN WITH GREYING BRISTLY HAIR, SWEPT FORWARD. HE HAD A TWINKLE TO HIS MANNER, BUT MICHEL GENERALLY FELL IN BEHIND HIS WIFE.

IN THE LITTLE HOUSE, CATHERINE AND I SHARED A BEDROOM. WE WENT TO BED AFTER DINNER, WHICH TO BE FAIR WAS ALWAYS DELICIOUS AND FEATURED LOCAL FOODS.

WE DRANK THE SPARKLY CRUDE CIDER FOR WHICH THE AREA IS FAMOUS. IT POPPED OUT OF ITS CHAMPAGNE BOTTLES TO FILL OUR GLASSES WITH A CLOUDY APPLE TREAT.

THE MEAL, WHICH GENERALLY INCLUDED A SALAD DRESSED WITH FINE CHIVES FROM THE GARDEN, A DELICATE CHICKEN AND LEEK SOUP, AND SOME KIND OF MEAT, WAS ALWAYS FINISHED BY A REGIONAL CHEESE, USUALLY A CAMEMBERT, WHICH I DID NOT LIKE AT FIRST, BUT LIKE SO MANY OTHER THINGS THAT SUMMER, I CAME TO LOVE.

THE FAMILY WERE JOINED BY THEIR PARIS NEIGHBORS, WHO SET UP CAMP IN THE GARDEN. THEY ENJOYED OFFERING ME NEW SENSATIONS OF TASTE.

THEY WATCHED ME WITH DELIGHT.

MY PIDGIN FRENCH TURNED RAPIDLY FLUENT AND MY FOREIGN TASTE FOLLOWED SUIT IN ITS HABITUDES.

OUR DAYS WERE EQUALLY PRESCRIBED.

AT SEVEN, WE WENT TO PLAY TENNIS AT THE LOCAL CLUB. THEN WE WOULD GO TO THE BEACH FOR CLUB SPORTIF.

WE EXERCISED AND LEARNED MARTIAL ARTS UNDER THE MOVIE STAR EYES OF OUR BRONZED TEACHER.

HE'D TRAINED THE AVENGERS OF TV FAME.

HE TAUGHT FIGHTING CHOREOGRAPHY TO MANY STARLETS

THE COAST OF NORMANDY IS NOT FAR FROM THE SOUTH COAST OF ENGLAND, AND IT IS NOT MUCH WARMER, EITHER.

THE SUN DID SHINE, BUT NOT ALWAYS.

OFTEN THE WIND BLEW ACROSS THE MILES OF SANDY DUNES, WHICH FORCED US TO WEAR SWEATERS AGAINST THE COLD.

AT NOON WHEN WE BEGAN OUR SWIM, THE SEA WAS OFTEN WARMER THAN THE AIR.

AS A STRONG SWIMMER, I ENJOYED THE LONG SOLITARY PULLS THROUGH THE WAVES...

LIKE MANY FRENCH CHILDREN, WE HAD PETS FOR THE SUMMER.

I WAS GIVEN A RABBIT TO NURTURE.

IT WAS TERRIFIED OF ME AND IT TOOK MANY DAYS AND ATTEMPTS BEFORE I WAS ABLE TO PET HIM.

WE MADE OUR BIDS IN TINY WAYS, LESS OBVIOUS THAN THE REBELLION OF THE RABBIT. WE WERE ALWAYS READY TO ESCAPE THE ADULT GAZE AND SOUGHT THE MEANS OF SIGNALLING EACH OTHER CONSTANTLY.

THE RABBIT'S DEFIANCE PRESENTED AN OPPORTUNITY.

...THE SALTY CARESS OF THE WAVES.

SOMETIMES MICHEL CAUGHT CREVETTES, TINY GREY SHRIMPS, DELICIOUS WHEN FRIED ALONGSIDE TINY CRUNCHY SPRATS.

IN THE AFTERNOONS THEY PUT THE FRYER OUTSIDE AND MADE THESE TREATS TO ACCOMPANY A NICE GLASS OF JOHNNY WALKER OR A PASTIS.

I HAD HORRIBLE WELTS WHERE HE RAVAGED MY ARMS AND THIGHS.

LIKE US, HE WAS DETERMINED TO ASSERT HIS FREE WILL.

WE USED HIM AS AN EXCUSE TO GO ON WALKS.

WE DAWDLED ON THE STRAGGLY DUNES, WAITING FOR HIM TO MOVE FORWARD.

HA HA HA
HA HA HA HA
HA

THE GRAVEL OF THE ROAD MINGLED WITH THE SAND THAT COLLECTED BY THE ROADSIDE.

WE WERE STUNG BY THE HIDDEN STONES IN THE GRAVEL.

TEENAGERS A FEW YEARS OUR SENIOR PASSED US WITH CREPES FROM THE STALL THAT CLUNG TO THE WINDY DRIVE ON THE EDGE OF THE WIDE EXPANSE OF THE SANDS.

AFTER AN HOUR OF DRAGGING LA BÊTE ALONG, WE WERE FRUSTRATED AND EXASPERATED.

WE WERE AS TETHERED AS THE RABBIT.

THERE WAS A FUTILITY TO OUR PROMENADE.

OH, LA VACHE!

J'EN AI MARRE, IT IS ENOUGH, NO?

TOMORROW, I'M GOING TO ASK OUTRIGHT IF WE CAN GO FOR A LITTLE WALK.

WHAT COULD SHE SAY BUT NO?

I CARRIED THE BEAUTIFUL BUT DIFFICULT CREATURE BACK.

BY NOW, THE EVENING CHILL HAD SET IN AND WE FELT THE PIQUE OF EACH STONE IN THE ROAD.

I WAS GLAD TO JOIN THE FAMILY AT THE TABLE FOR THE WARM EVENING MEAL AND THE COMPANY.

CHILDHOOD SLIPPED ON AND OFF ME SO EASILY THAT YEAR.

WHEN THE DINNER WAS OVER WE MADE LITTLE SHOWS, WITH SONGS AND MIMES, WHILE THE ADULTS ENJOYED A GLASS OF SOMETHING.

WE WERE COZY IN THE LITTLE HOUSE.

SHORTLY AFTER THE FIRST WEEK, THE NEIGHBORS ARRIVED WITH THEIR TWO SONS. BEST RECORD THIS WEEK, LAST WEEK, BEST MOVIE, MOVIE STAR, THE SHALLOWNESS OF ADULTS, AND MUCH FEIGNING OF DISINTEREST.

THEY HAD DOGS, ONE THAT SCARED MY RABBIT.

CAN'T YOU KEEP HIM AWAY FROM TANGY?

I BONDED WITH THE BIG EYES THAT SPOKE MUTELY TO ME.

THE ANIMAL, THOUGH EMOTIONALLY DETACHED FROM ME, WAS IN MY CARE AND I IDENTIFIED WITH IT AND TRIED TO KEEP IT SAFE.

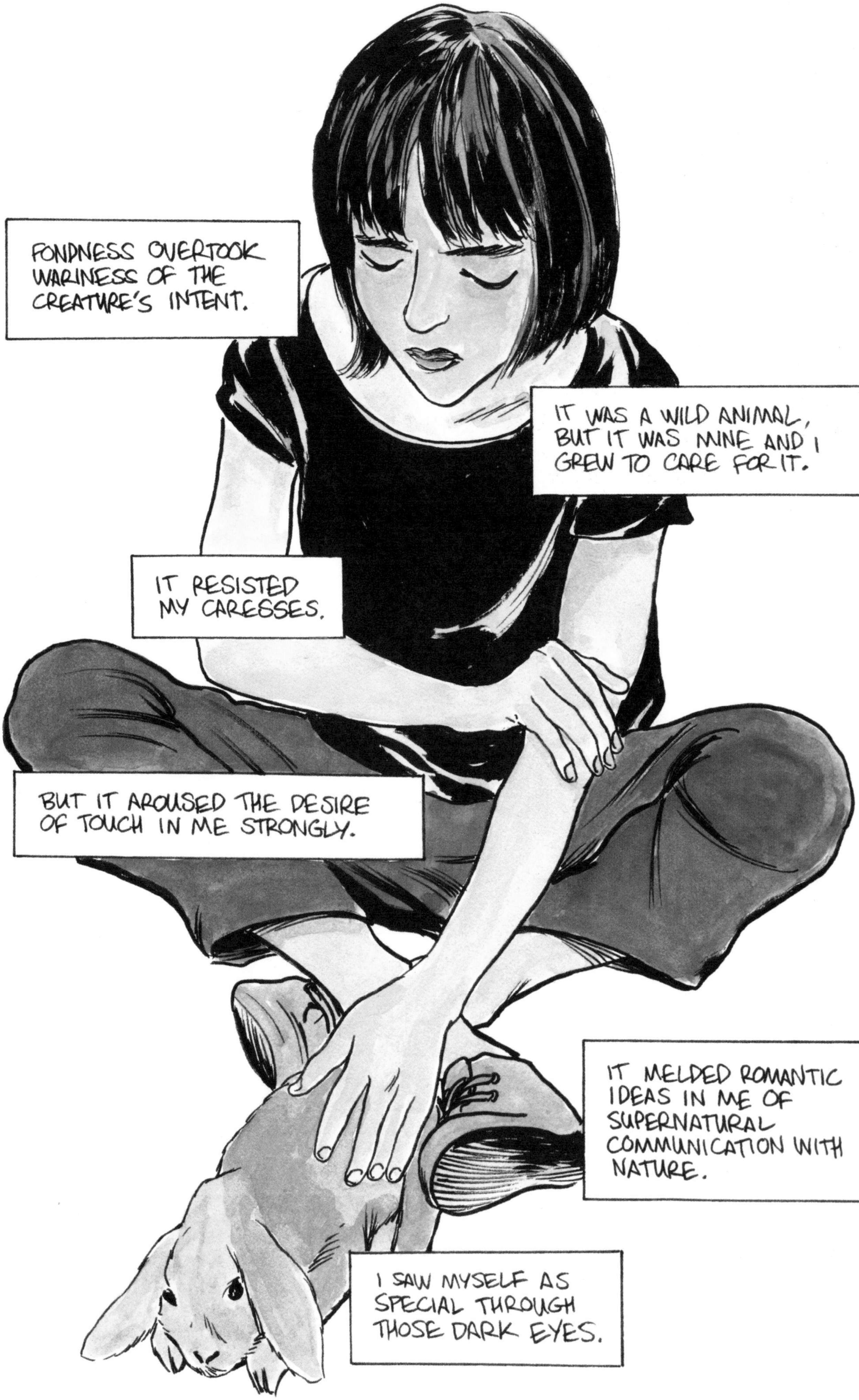
FONDNESS OVERTOOK WARINESS OF THE CREATURE'S INTENT.
IT WAS A WILD ANIMAL, BUT IT WAS MINE AND I GREW TO CARE FOR IT.
IT RESISTED MY CARESSES.
BUT IT AROUSED THE DESIRE OF TOUCH IN ME STRONGLY.
IT MELDED ROMANTIC IDEAS IN ME OF SUPERNATURAL COMMUNICATION WITH NATURE.
I SAW MYSELF AS SPECIAL THROUGH THOSE DARK EYES.

SOON THE BOYS CAME OVER THE WALL LESS AND LESS.

THEY WERE PHILISTINES.

THEY DID NOT UNDERSTAND BEAUTY OR THE ROMANTIC.

THEY DESPISED POETRY, AND THEY PLAYED FOOTBALL.

MAMMAN, CAN WE GO FOR A PETITE TOUR?

JUST AS FAR AS THE BEACH.

WE ARE BORING OURSELVES HERE.

CATHERINE IMPLEMENTED OUR TEMPORARILY SUSPENDED PLAN.

OH, WHY NOT, CHERIE?

LET THEM GO FOR A LITTLE WHILE.

HER MOTHER OPENED HER MOUTH TO REFUSE, BUT MICHEL WAS MELTED.

LIKE A MIRACLE, THE NEIGHBORS SHOOED US OFF TOO, AND YVONNE HAD NO TIME TO OBJECT.

MICHEL SLAPPED HER ROUND BIKINIED BOTTOM.

SWAK

SHE BLUSHED, DISTRACTED MOMENTARILY.

145

OUR ESPADRILLES FLOPPED SILENTLY IN THE DUST.

NOW ON THE BEACH, THE SANDY SHORES BELONGED TO US. THE WATER SPREAD OUT BEFORE US, THE DULL BLUE OF THE CHANNEL. FEW PEOPLE REMAINED ON THE LEES.

THE WATER GLISTENED IN SHALLOW FRILLS OVER THE SAND. MY MIND FLEW TO THE HORIZON AND I BREATHED THE FIRST DEEP BREATHS OF ADULTHOOD.

IN THE FREEDOM, AN INVISIBLE FORCE CAME TO ME AND COURSED OVER MY BODY.

HA HA HA HA

HA HA HA HA HA

I SPLATTERED WATER IN ARCS, AND THE SAND GLINTED WHERE MY WEIGHT MOISTENED THE MUD.

AS THE SUN BEGAN TO LEAVE THE SKY...

AND THE TOURISTS BEGAN TO TURN ON THEIR RADIOS, OPEN WINE, AND BUILD FIRES, WE MADE OUR WAY BACK.

WARY OF CRUDE CIVILIZATION, WE BARELY LINGERED.

BUT I WAS STOPPED IN MY TRACKS BY THE SIGHT OF A BEAUTIFUL BOY; HIS CHÂTAIN HAIR FELL OVER HIS PERFECT FACE.

WHAT WAS THIS ICON DOING AT THE EDGE OF THE BANAL WORLD?

THERE WAS NO CONVERSATION OF NOTE.

BUT THERE I SAW HIM AND HE SAW ME. HE WAS SWEET AND SOFT-SPOKEN.

JEAN MICHEL PROMISED TO SEE ME IN THE MORNING IF I COULD SLIP AWAY FOR A FEW MINUTES FROM THE TENNIS CLUB.

INTO THE WOODS, PERHAPS?

I WILL

THE NEXT MORNING, HE WAS THERE AT THE PERIMETER OF THE CLUB.

I WENT INTO THE PINES ALONG THE FENCE.

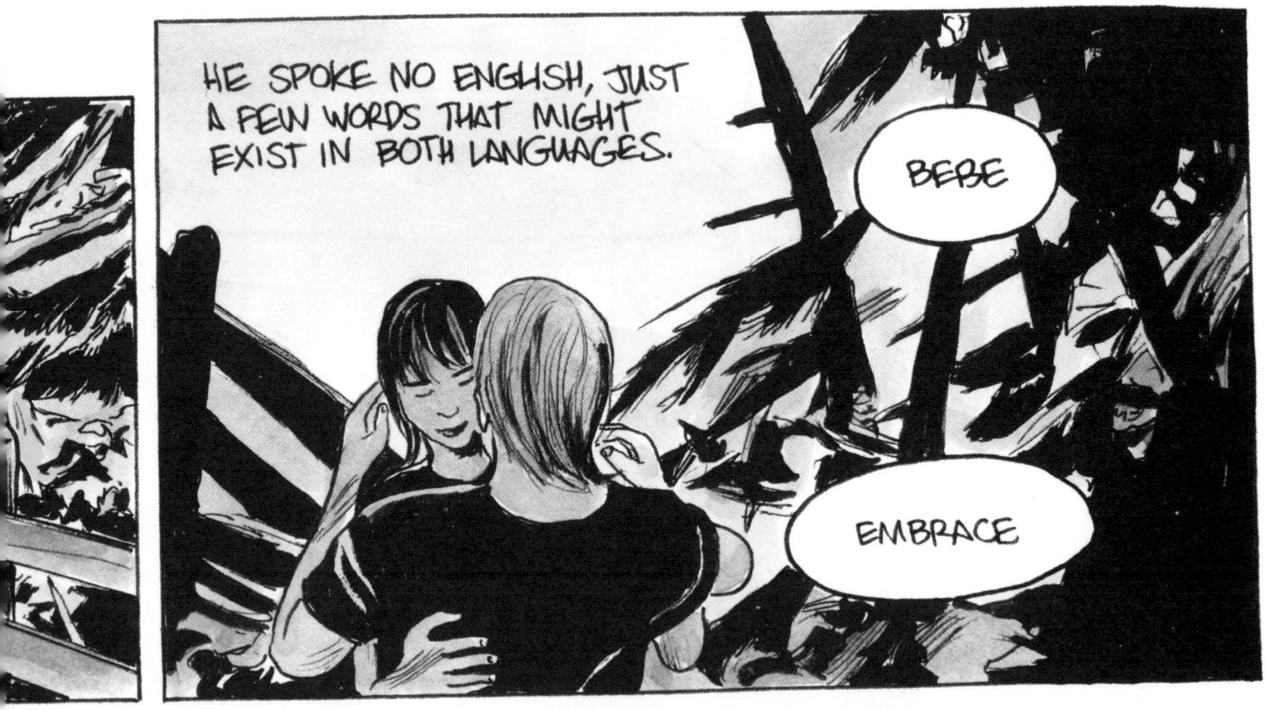
HE SPOKE NO ENGLISH, JUST A FEW WORDS THAT MIGHT EXIST IN BOTH LANGUAGES.
BEBE
EMBRACE

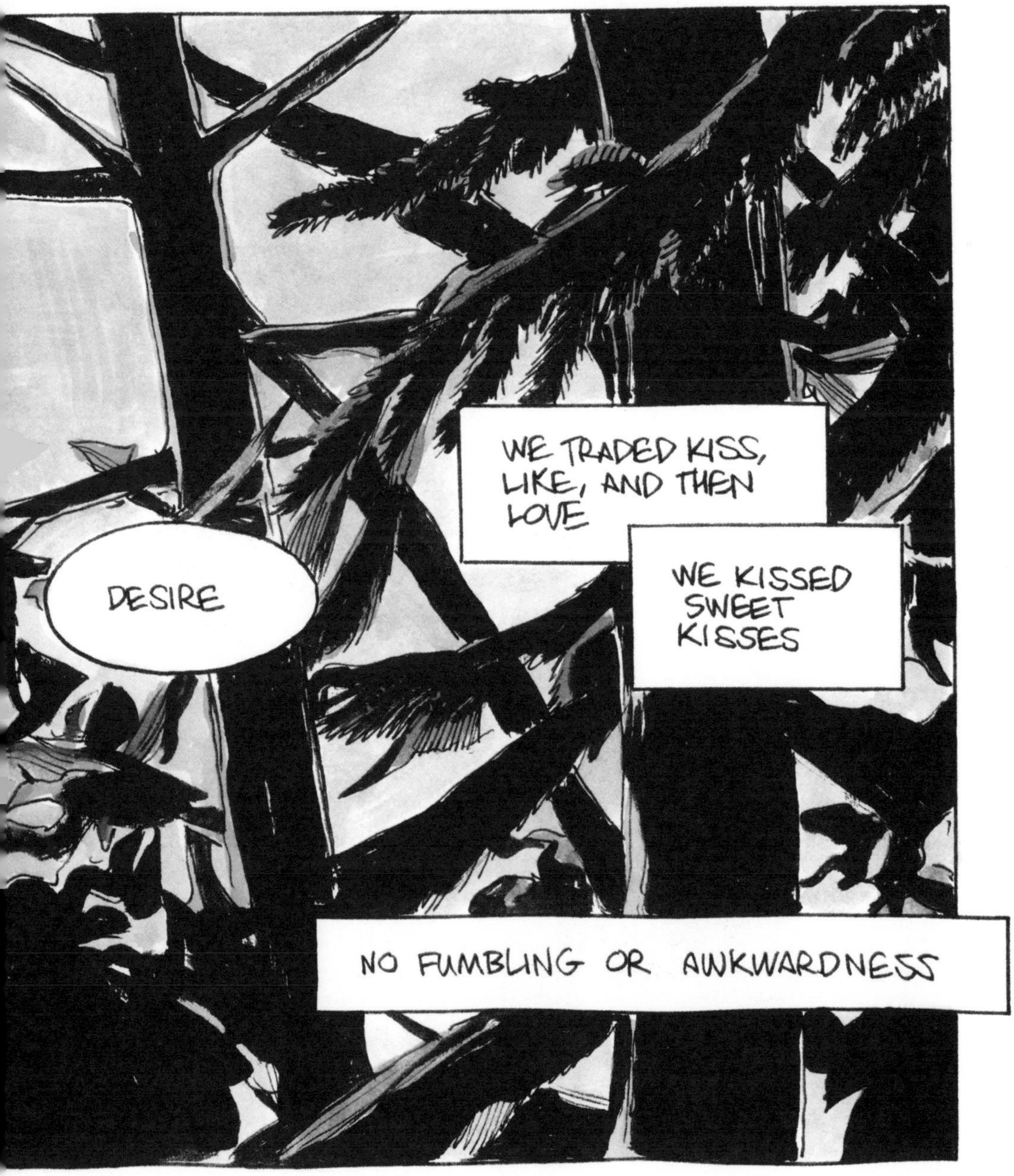
WE TRADED KISS, LIKE, AND THEN LOVE
DESIRE
WE KISSED SWEET KISSES
NO FUMBLING OR AWKWARDNESS

ALL TOO SOON, HE WAS GONE AWAY OVER THE DUNES THAT BANKED THE PINES.

CATHERINE FINISHED HER GAME, THEN LAUGHING, WE RAN HOME TO CHANGE FOR THE BEACH.

THESE LITTLE RENDEZVOUS SNATCHED ON THE SIDE OF THE ROAD HAPPENED 2 OR 3 TIMES MORE AND THEN HE LEFT, BACK TO WHEREVER HE HAD COME FROM.

THEY WERE DIFFICULT TO ACCOMPLISH BECAUSE YVONNE WOULD SECRETLY WATCH US. I HATED THE INTRUSION. THERE WAS SOMETHING MEAN ABOUT THE WAY SHE SOUGHT US OUT.

IT WAS NOT TO SEE IF WE WERE OKAY, BUT RATHER TO PROVE THAT WE WERE NOT TO BE TRUSTED AND TO CONFIRM OUR VENAL NATURE, AS IF WE WOULD DO SOMETHING BASE OR UNFORGIVABLE.

BUT WE ONLY WANTED TO BE PART OF THE ROMANCE OF LIFE.

OUR TRANSGRESSIONS WERE AS SWEET AS THOSE THAT FROSTED A PLUM.

THAT SUMMER I PLANNED TO WRITE TO HIM AND I BELIEVED HE WOULD WRITE TO ME. HE GAVE ME HIS PICTURE AND I WAS IN LOVE. BROWN EYES AGAINST FAIR BROWN HAIR ARE NORMAN TRAITS THAT MELT MY HEART, QUALITIES MY RABBIT SHARED WITH MY BOYFRIEND.

BOTH ARE ONLY TO BE KEPT FOR THE SUMMER.

THOUGH, THOSE SUMMERS FELT NEVER-ENDING.

FEAST DAYS PUNCTUATED OUR SÉJOURS, AND WE WOULD ALL PILE INTO THE CAR TO GLIDE AWAY FROM THE SEA INTO THE NORMAN COUNTRYSIDE, WHERE YVONNE'S MOTHER HAD A FARM.

WE PULLED UP THE LANE INTO THE CLEARING TO FIND OURSELVES BEFORE THE LONG LOW FERME. IT WAS AN ANCIENT HEAP.

THE BARN DOORS WERE WIDE OPEN AND THE SOUND OF COWS ESCAPED FROM THE SHADOWS INSIDE.

CATHERINE'S GRANDMOTHER MEMERE RESEMBLED HER DAUGHTER.

BUT WHERE YVONNE HAD ALL THE POLISH OF THE WIFE OF A SUCCESSFUL PARISIAN, MEMERE RETAINED ALL THE MANNER OF THE RUSTIC IN HER APRON AND SLIPPERS, HER HAIR WILD AND BURNT FROM SOME OLD PERM.

WE WOULD EMBRACE HER AND HER BROTHER AND THEN AT LEAST ANOTHER TWENTY FAMILY MEMBERS.

...WHO WOULD ALL SOON BE SITTING CLOSE TOGETHER AT THE DINING BOARD.

WE CHILDREN WERE NOT EXPECTED TO JOIN THEM JUST YET. WE WERE TAKEN TO SEE THE DUCKS AND GEESE AND THE HUTCHES, BIRTHPLACE OF MY OWN RABBIT.

THE FARM WAS A WORKING FARM; ITS ROUGH EDGES CAME FROM USE AND CONSTANT WEAR IN THE BATTLE WITH THE ELEMENTS.

THE YARD WAS FRAMED WITH STRAGGLING TIRED GREY APPLE TREES. THEY LOOKED WRUNG OUT FROM USE. NO EFFORT WAS MADE TO CONCEAL THE DAILY COMPOST.

THE GOAL HERE WAS FUNCTION, NOT BEAUTY, AND THE MIDDLE-CLASS VALUES OF PROPRIETY GAVE WAY TO THE NEEDS OF THE ANIMALS: DAILY TASKS LIKE MILKING AND CHEESE-MAKING, AND THE PRODUCTION OF APPLE CIDER.

NO PICTURESQUE COTTAGE, THIS FARM BREATHED A BOOZY WARM WELCOME ACROSS THE LANDSCAPE.

THE SMELL OF CURDLED MILK HUNG ABOUT IT LIKE BABY BREATH.

THE HOUSE WAS NOT A SUNNY PLACE WITH SHIMMERING POTS; RATHER ALL THE PANS THAT HUNG ABOUT THE OVENS AND CHIMNEY WERE BLACK FROM USE.

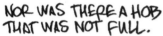

NOR WAS THERE A HOB THAT WAS NOT FULL.

OR A CORNER WHERE SOME STONEWARE DID NOT SIT COVERED WITH MUSLIN TO PROTECT ITS CONTENTS FROM FLIES.

A TABLE, LES ENFANTS, A TABLE!

VENEZ LES FILLES!

EVERY AVAILABLE SURFACE INDOORS AND OUT WAS IN THE SERVICE OF SOME CULINARY DELICACY.

WE WERE PULLED OUT OF THE SUN.

INTO THE DARK OF THE HIGH-CEILINGED KITCHEN.

IN SECONDS WE WERE SQUEEZED BETWEEN HAPPY FRENCHMEN, RELATIVES WHO NOW DID WHAT THEY WERE BORN TO DO.

EAT AND DRINK

IT WAS NOON WHEN WE BEGAN.

THEY WERE AMUSED BY MY ENGLISH ACCENT AND INQUIRED ABOUT MY FAMILY.

C'EST DU BON, NON?

"GOÛTEZ-TASTE" BECAME THE IMPERATIVE FROM THEN ON. FIRST CAME SAUCISSON, SLICES OF SAUSAGE, HARD, CHEWY, DELICIOUS. ONE, TWO THREE TYPES, SOME SMALL, SOME FAT.

THEY WANTED TO KNOW, BUT THEY WERE LAUGHING AND ASKING EACH OTHER QUESTIC

THE BREAD WAS PULLED AND PASSED.

THE GLASSES WERE FILLED WITH THE DUSKY CIDER POURED FROM BOTTLES WIPED FREE OF THE BARN DIRT ONLY SECONDS BEFORE,

FROM THERE, MUSSELS APPEARED IN GIANT TUREENS, DOTTED WITH SHALLOTS PICKED FROM THE GARDEN FENCE, SWIMMING IN WINE AND BUTTER.

THEY RELEASED THEIR PARFUM IN THE MISTS RISING FROM THE POTS.

HA HA HA HA HA

WE EAT ROAST BIF... FOR OUR VACANCES.

I RESPONDED AS BEST I COULD.

LAUGHTER AND KNOWING LOOKS ABOUT ENGLISH FOOD OVERTOOK THE TABLE.

MEMERE, DID YOU MAKE THIS?

NO, DIDIER BOUGHT IT FROM LON. WHAT DO YOU THINK?

AH, OUI, CA VA.

THIS WAS NOT GONE FROM OUR PLATES WHEN THE GRAISSE OF RILLETTES WAS PIERCED FOR SERVING.

THIS ITEM MEMERE HAD MADE FROM SCRATCH. ITS COARSE THREADS OF PORK MELTED WITH THE FAT THAT ENCLOSED IT.

AND WINES, RED WINES, WHITE WINES, UN GOÛT, UN SOUPÇON, UN VINTAGE SPECTACULAR, WE TASTED AND TRIED TOO.

THEN THE FOIE GRAS AND THE PÂTÉS PASSED FROM COARSE TO THE FINEST TEXTURES.

IN MOUSSES WHIPPED FROM THE COOL CLOUDS ABOVE AND ANCHORED WITH EARTHY WARM COGNACS.

PEOPLE LEANT FORWARD AND SUCKED AND SAVORED.

IT SEEMED AS THOUGH THE SUNLIGHT WAS ONLY THERE TO HIGHLIGHT THE ENORMOUS PLATTERS THAT WERE SET BEFORE US, ONE AFTER THE OTHER.

THEN, CREVETTES, PILED IN A FRENZY OF TINY CLAWS.

THEY WERE LURED FROM THE STREAMS NEARBY BY MICHEL AND THE OTHER MEN WITH A SMALL PIECE OF RED MEAT ON A STRING.

FROM THERE IT IS ONLY A MOMENT UNTIL THEY ARE IN THE POT.

THE HUNTERS TOOK PRIDE IN THE SERVING.

AH, MICHEL, HE KNOWS ALL THE BEST CORNERS TO FIND THEM.

THE CROWD WAS TOLD OF THE LOCATION AND THE PLENITUDE, ALL OF WHICH BROUGHT OUT CHILDHOOD STORIES OF BITES AND NIPS AND SOME SMALL EMBARRASSMENTS, USUALLY ABOUT GETTING CAUGHT WITH ONE'S PANTS DOWN.

THE BEASTIES WERE EATEN DRIPPING IN UNSALTED BUTTER.

IT REMINDED ONE OF THE GRASSY MEADOWS WHERE THE COWS FED.

THE COST OF THEIR CAPTURE ADDED TO THEIR FLAVOR AS WE SUCKED OUT THE HOLLOW SHELLS.

THE COMPANY SALTED THE FOOD TO PERFECTION.

SEVERAL HOURS PASSED IN HAPPY SOCIABILITY AND THE SAVORY OF THE OPENING OFFERINGS WERE ERASED FROM THE PALATE WITH A PLATE OF CLEANSING BOILED LEEK. THE VEGETABLE THEME WAS CONSOLIDATED BY A HEARTY RATATOUILLE.

NOW CAME THE BIRDS

CONFIT DE CANARD   POULET RÔTI   COQUELETS

DRESSED AND SERVED WITH SAUCES AND CRÈMES.

MEATS THAT I DID NOT KNOW WERE PUT BEFORE ME AND I ATE EACH TASTY MORSEL BELIEVING IT MUST BE THE LAST.

IT NEVER WAS.

THOUGH DELICIOUS, THE SHEER VOLUME AND NUMBER OF DISHES BEGAN TO OVERWHELM ME.

THIS MEAT WHEN TOUCHED FELL APART.

ITS TENDERNESS EMITTED A SCENT OF LAVENDER FROM THE HERBS THAT IMBUED ITS SUBTLE JUICES.

CATHERINE'S UNCLE TONTON THREW A FEW SCRAPS TO THE DOGS AT THE DOOR.

THE COTTAGE WAS FILLED WITH THE BLISSFUL VAPOR OF THE MANY OFFERINGS.

NOW CAME THE POT-AU-FEU, TO APPLAUSE.

THE VEGETABLES, WHICH PERFUMED THE MEAT, LAY NESTLING AROUND IT, THEIR STRINGS USED TO PULL THEM FROM THE POT WHEN THEY WERE AT THEIR PERFECT TEXTURE, AND HELD THEM IN A SORT OF EROTIC RELATION TO THE BOILED BEEF THAT REIGNED OVER THE OTHER CHARCUTERIE.

DOMES OF CABBAGE GLISTENED LIKE MULTIPLE ST. PETERS TO THE MITER OF BEEF.

THEY BATHED THE PLATES, A MIRACLE OF GOLDEN CLARITY.

AS ALL THIS GASTRONOMY PROGRESSED, THE COMPANY POURED WINES AND SMOKED AND SWEATED AND SMILED.

NO ONE MADE TO MOVE OR THOUGHT TO GO ANYWHERE.

AT 4:30, A SLIGHT PAUSE FOR A CIGAR OR A PIPE, A QUICK PEEPEE AND THEN THEY WERE READY FOR THE GIGOT.

MICHEL BORE THE LEG OF LAMB FROM THE RÔTI OVER THE FIRE OUTSIDE.

159

IT SEEMED PAGAN, WITH ITS ROSEMARY SPRIGS STICKING FROM THE BONDAGE OF ITS TIES LIKE A ROMAN CROWN, ITS SIDES LANCED AND STUFFED WITH GARLIC CLOVES.

A PUREE WAS BESIDE THE SLICES THAT WERE PLACED REVERENTLY BEFORE US.

AT SOME POINT THE WHOLE AFTERNOON BLURRED TOGETHER.

AS QUICHES AND PIES WERE REPLACED BY CHEESES AND CREAMS.

BEATEN PAST THE STURDINESS OF ANGLO MASH, THE POTATOES TOOK ON A CREAMY DECADENCE,

PULLED BY THE CIDER AND FOOD, WE GIRLS SAT STUPEFIED AND HORRIFIED BY THE RELENTLESSNESS OF THE CONTINUED FEAST.

AT HALF PAST FIVE, YVONNE COMMANDED US OUTSIDE TO WALK SO THAT WE COULD MAKE ROOM FOR DESSERT.

WE ESCAPED GRATEFULLY INTO THE SUNLIGHT AND FRESH AIR.

AGAIN FREE OF THE ADULT GAZE, WE WALKED WITH LADEN STOMACHS.

NOW IN THE EARLY EVENING OF THE FALL, THE CRICKETS BEGAN TO SING AND THE WIND BLEW GENTLY THROUGH THE ORCHARDS.

WE PASSED A MAN WITH A CALVADOS STILL.

DESPITE OUR AGE, HE OFFERED US A SIP.

IT BURNED MY TONGUE AND THROAT.

MY EYES WATERED.

DRINK TOO MUCH OF IT BEFORE IT HAS MATURED AND YOU CAN GO BLIND.

IT DIDN'T SIT WELL ON THE ROILING FOOD IN OUR STOMACHS. OUR PACE WAS SLUGGISH. THE SUN WAS TOO HOT.

WE MARCHED ALONG THE TARMAC.

AFTER A WHILE WE CAME TO AN OLD CHURCH.

WE ENTERED ITS COOL INTERIOR.

SO I LAY DOWN.

I COULDN'T EVEN LAY ON MY BACK.

IT'S TIME FOR DESSERT!

REALLY, YOU GIRLS ARE RIDICULOUS.

WE DID NOT TELL HER ABOUT THE CALVADOS UNTIL MUCH LATER, WHEN THE MEMORY OF THE DAY HAD PASSED INTO FAMILY LEGEND.

BACK AT THE FARM, SINGING AND DRINKING GAMES HAD TAKEN OVER,

THE SMELL OF THE POLISHED WOOD AND INCENSE SOOTHED OUR OVERLOADED SENSES,

I TRIED TO SIT AT ONE OF THE PEWS,

WE GROPED OUR WAY THROUGH THE DARKNESS

BUT BENDING CAUSED MY TUMMY TO BE CONSTRICTED.

IT WAS NECESSARY TO LAY ON MY SIDE TO SUPPORT MY BULGING TUMMY.

GET UP!

IN THE THROES OF ANGRY DIGESTION, THE DOORS OPENED RUDELY AND YVONNE ENTERED.

GET UP, COME ON!

WHAT'RE YOU DOING?

SPECTACULAR POTS OF CHOCOLATE MOUSSE APPEARED NEXT TO A PERFECTLY RINGED APPLE TART.

CLOUDS OF UNSWEETENED MERINGUES FLOATED IN CUSTARD. WE CUT AND PEELED PEARS, PEACHES, APPLES, AND GRAPES, EACH SWEETER THAN THE LAST.

ALL WITH CHAMPAGNE
AND TINY COFFEES.

SUGAR LUMPS WERE DUNKED AND
SUCKED WITH BISCOTTIS AND CAKES,
MADELEINES MET WITH BABAS.

THE SMELL OF HUMANITY REPLACED THE DELICATE SCENTS OF THE DAY
WITH SWEAT AND GARLIC, GAS AND LIQUOR, BUT FOR A MOMENT WE
FORGOT BEAUTY AND JOINED MORE IMMEDIATE PLEASURE.

FINALLY, WE FELL
INTO OUR COTS
AT KINKOW...

INTO THE
UNCOMFORTABLE
BUT HEAVY
SLEEP OF
INDIGESTION.

IN THE MORNING,
PEOPLE MOVED
SLOWLY.

TISANE
DOES YOU
GOOD.

YVONNE WAS READY FOR
THE MOMENT WHEN SHE
COULD RETURN TO BED
FOR THE DAY.

THE DARK SETTLED AROUND THE HOUSE AS IF THE NIGHT TOO WAS ENJOYING THE FEAST AND PEEKING IN THE WINDOWS.

FOOD AND LOVE GO TOGETHER...

THE COMMUNION OF THE EVENING WITH SONGS, FAMILY AND SATIETY.

AFTER AFFECTIONATE GOODBYES, WE FINALLY DROVE BACK THROUGH THE DARK LANES, FOLLOWING THE NARROW FOCUS OF THE HEADLIGHTS BEFORE US.

ALL THE WHILE, WE WISHED WE WERE HOME.

AND OFF WE WENT TO OUR BEACH CLUB AND OUR LITTLE ROMANCES WITH PRETTY BOYS WITH WHOM WE FLIRTED FROM AFAR...

AND THE CLEANSING SHUSH OF THE SEA AIR.

IT WAS NEARING THE END OF THE SUMMER WHEN WE VISITED MEMERE AGAIN.

MY RABBIT HAD TO GO TO BE WITH HIS BROTHERS AND SISTERS.

WE PLAYED AROUND THE BARN AND WENT INTO THE ORCHARDS, SPAT OUT APPLES TOO SHARP FOR EATING AND CHASED THE DUCKS.

CATHERINE HAD GONE OFF WITH HER COUSIN BRIGITTE FOR A TARTINE.

COME OUT, MARGUERITE.

SAY GOODBYE TO YOUR RABBIT!

YVONNE BIT HER LIP, ALMOST AS IF IN ANTICIPATION OF PLEASURE.

DON'T HOLD HIM BY THE EARS!!

YOU'LL HURT HIM!!

TANGY'S SCREAM LASTED FOR SECONDS AS MEMERE CUT UP HIS GUT TO HIS NECK.

SHE TUCKED THE BLADE IN HER APRON AND WITH HER NEWLY FREED HAND PULLED MY PET'S INSIDES FROM ITS BODY.

THEY SLIPPED TO THE GROUND WHERE THE DOG BEGAN TO EAT THEM HAPPILY.

HE LOOKED AT ME ONCE WITH
A GRATEFUL BLOODY FACE.

I-I DIDN'T
KNOW.

BEFORE MEMERE
SHOOED HIM OFF.

I DID NOT CRY. I WAS TOO SHAKEN AND TOO POLITE
TO CRITICIZE MY HOSTS.

I RETREATED WITH MY THOUGHTS
FOR THE REST OF THE TRIP BACK
TO THE SEASIDE.

I SHOULD HAVE KNOWN THAT
THIS WAS THE LOGICAL OUTCOME.

I FELT FOOLISH ABOUT THE AFFECTION
I HAD SHOWN THE ANIMAL.

IT SEEMED THAT
THINGS MUST CHANGE.

THE ADULT WORLD
WAS BARBAROUS.

I BEGAN TO RECONSTRUCT MY ROMANTIC EXCLUSIVE
VIEW OF THE WORLD, THOUGH NOW I WAS A LITTLE LESS
PURE THAN WHEN THE SEASON BEGAN.

AS AUGUST DREW TO AN END,
WE WORE OUR JEANS EVERY
EVENING AGAINST THE CHILL
OF THE SEA AIR THAT SWEPT
ALONG THE BEACH.

AND CLOSED THE
SHUTTERS TO KEEP
THE HEAT FROM
THE STOVE INSIDE.

THE SOUP TASTED BETTER IN THE COOL OF SUNDOWN, AND THE BLACK OF NIGHT CLOSED IN EARLIER.

PARIS BECKONED US BACK

UPON OUR RETURN TO THE CITY, WE BEGAN TO WEAR A LITTLE LIPSTICK, NOW WITH YUONNE'S APPROVAL, AND WE ADOPTED THE MANNERS OF THE PARISIENNE.

WE SHOPPED FOR THE FIRST FEW DAYS.

WE CAUGHT UP WITH THE LATEST RECORD RELEASES AND SAT AROUND IN SIDEWALK CAFES.

CATHERINE AND I WAITED RESIGNEDLY TO RETURN SHORTLY TO SCHOOL AND SAY GOODBYE UNTIL THE NEXT HOLIDAYS.

IN THE EVENINGS, DINNER WAS A LITTLE MORE FORMAL.

THE GLASSES WERE CRYSTAL AND THE PLATES CHINA.

THE PARENTS ALLOWED A TASTE OF WHATEVER WINE WAS BEING SERVED, ALTHOUGH WE STILL PREFERRED THE MUSKY CIDER THAT MICHEL BROUGHT BACK BY THE CASE LOAD.

THE CULINARY TROPHIES FROM NORMANDY WERE EATEN WITH A THOUGHTFUL RELISH.

THE TASTE OF CERTAIN THINGS BROUGHT A RUSTIC INVIGORATION AND TACITLY RECOGNIZED SETS OF SENSES WERE INVOLVED, THROUGH THE PLEASURE OF A BIT OF PÂTÉ.

THEN ONE EVENING, THEY PREPARED A STEW OF SORTS.

IT SEEMED A GOOD CHOICE AGAINST THE FALL CHILL.

I ATE THE SWEET MEAT AND ENJOYED THE FLESH AS IT FELL FROM THE BONES.

WHAT IS THIS?

I DIDN'T RECOGNIZE THE BONES' FORM IMMEDIATELY.

IT'S RABBIT.

YVONNE LOOKED TO SEE HOW I WOULD REACT.

IT'S GOOD.

DO YOU WANT SOME MORE?

YES.

I HELD OUT MY PLATE.

THE RABBIT WAS COOKED IN A DELICIOUS TOMATO RAGOUT...
...IT WAS DELECTABLE.

I KNEW IT WAS MY RABBIT.

IS THIS THE RABBIT FROM THE FARM?

AND I EVEN VENTURED TO ASK...

YES.

AND SO IT WAS I ATE MY PET AND REMEMBERED ALL OF THE FUN TIMES OF THE SUMMER.

I UNDERSTOOD THE NORMAN WIND AND THE STORIES I HAD READ BY MAUPASSANT, WHICH THOUGH THEY HAD ONCE HORRIFIED ME, NOW MADE SENSE. FROM THE BETRAYAL I TOOK A LITTLE PRAGMATISM OF MY OWN.

THIS WAS THE SEASON WHEN I REALIZED THAT I MUST LEAVE MY LOVES BEHIND.

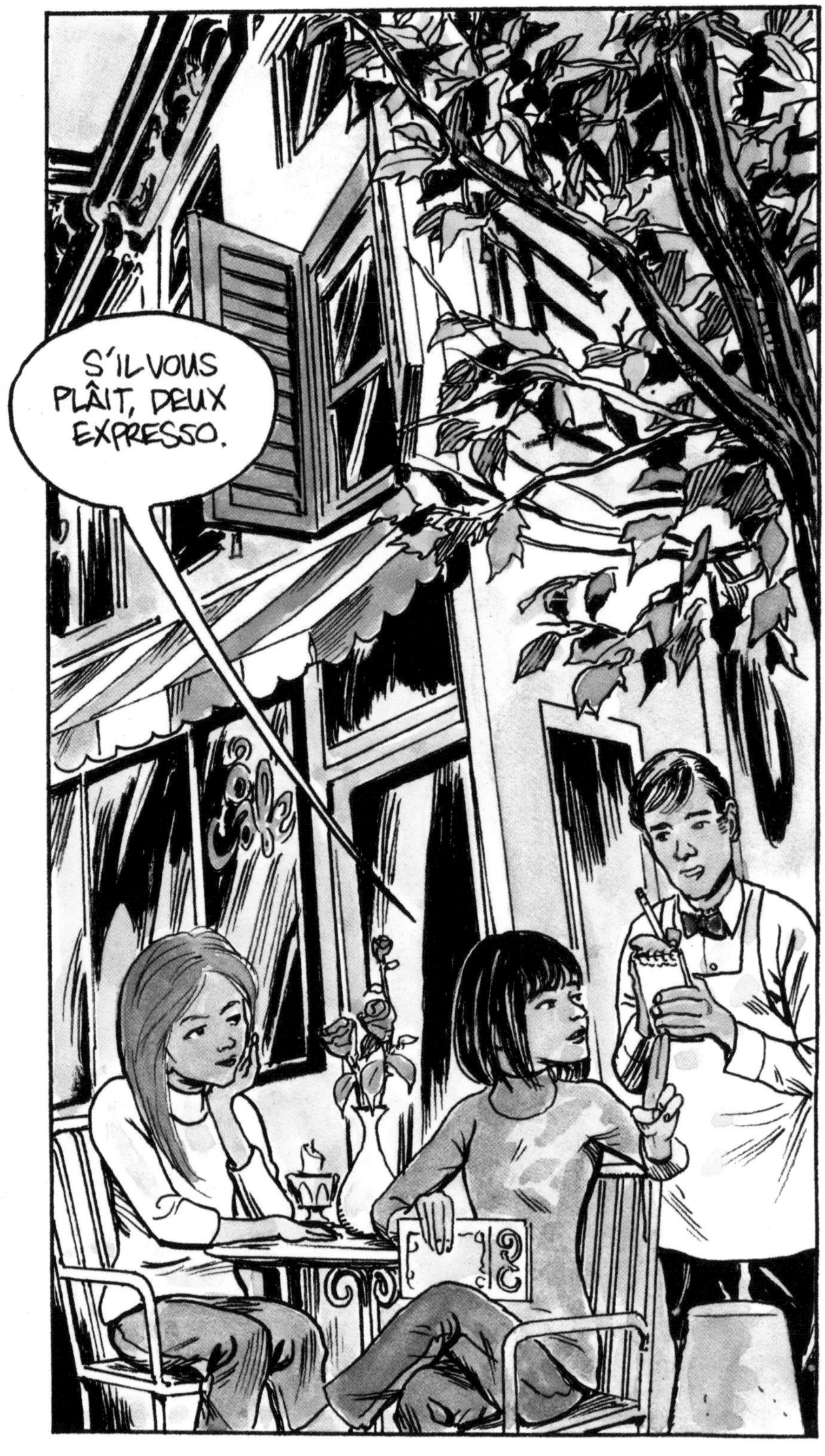
S'IL VOUS PLÂIT, DEUX EXPRESSO.

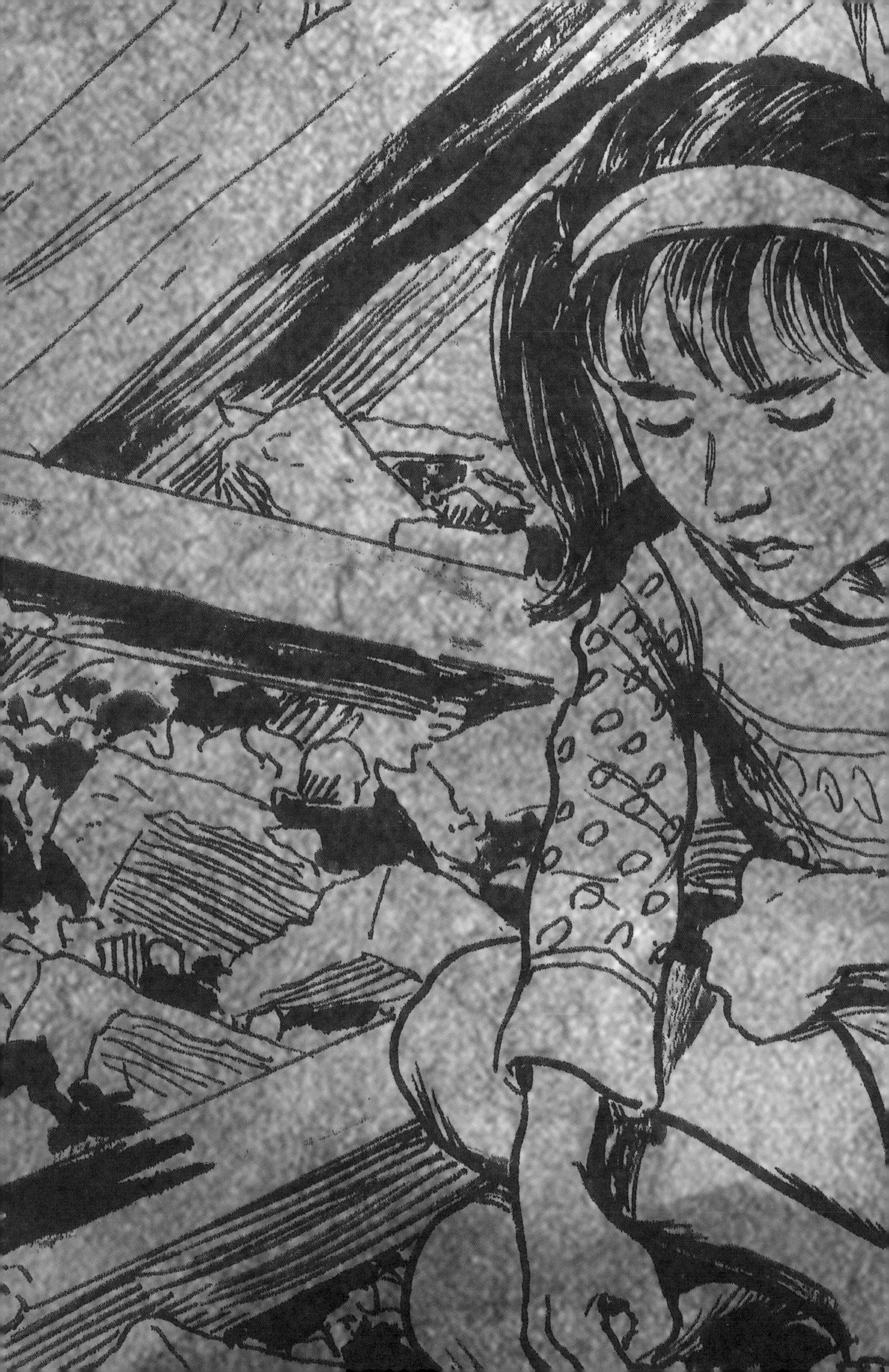